My Say

A Mentor's Guide to Success

My Say

A Mentor's Guide to Success

Edwin E. Bobrow

Chandler House Press
Worcester, Massachusetts
1999

My Say: A Mentor's Guide to Success

Copyright © 1999 by Edwin E. Bobrow

ISBN 1-886284-36-9
Library of Congress Catalog Card Number 98-89738
First Edition
ABCDEFGHIJK

Published by
Chandler House Press
335 Chandler Street
Worcester, MA 01602
USA

President Lawrence J. Abramoff

Publisher/Editor-in-Chief Richard J. Staron

Director of Retail Sales and Marketing Claire Cousineau Smith

Editorial/Production Manager Jennifer J. Goguen

Book Design Bookmakers

Cover Design Marshall Henrichs

Chandler House Press books are available at special discounts for bulk purchases. For more information about how to arrange such purchases, please contact Chandler House Press, 335 Chandler Street, Worcester, MA 01602, or call (800) 642-6657, or fax (508) 756-9425, or find us on the World Wide Web at www.tatnuck.com.

Chandler House Press books are distributed to the trade by
National Book Network, Inc.
4720 Boston Way
Lanham, MD 20706
(800) 462-6420

To Gloria
My wife, my friend, my soulmate

CONTENTS

ACKNOWLEDGMENTS

Dick Staron, publisher and editor-in-chief of Chandler House Press, suggested the concept for *My Say: A Mentor's Guide to Success*. He guided me through the writing, as he has guided me for the past 23 years as my primary editor and publisher. Dick is unique in the world of publishing today: He is extremely creative and knows the publishing business inside out. I am proud to call him my friend and to have had the privilege of working with him over the years—he has been a great teacher.

Dick, a big thanks for always being there and for being the grandfather of My Say.

There is one person, my wife, Gloria, without whom I could never have written any of my books or articles. Gloria took the working title of the book, "My Say," and added "A Mentor's Guide to Success" so that the title became a true reflection of the book. Her ideas, concepts, research, and meticulous editing of all my works, which she carries out with great patience and integrity, can never receive sufficient thanks. I can't imagine life without her or any writing of mine without her input.

Gloria, my deep thanks for being my partner and for always being there for me.

Thanks, too, to friends, colleagues, students, and family who shared their ideas of success. Without their input and what I have learned from my Dad, teachers, mentors, my son Mark, my brother David, and my students, I could never have had the success in life that I now enjoy.

I thank you all.

—Ed Bobrow

INTRODUCTION

Dick Staron, publisher and editor-in-chief of Chandler House Press, conceived and helped develop this book. He believed that sharing the lessons I have learned over a lifetime might be of help to those of you seeking "success" for yourselves. I am grateful to him not only for the opportunity, but because I was forced to review the successes and failures of my life's journey. Dick and I talked about how to best share my failures and successes and the lessons I learned from them. He suggested I describe actual experiences, and then give you the guides and rules I have come to live by—the guides and rules that have helped me and many others achieve success. I also included work forms I developed to use as guides in planning well and as an aid for the actions that will lead to your personal success.

Everyone wants success! Here, finally, is a book that talks about success in realistic terms—from the lessons I learned in achieving my success to defining the many faces of success and how to determine what success is for each of you. You will learn how to appraise abilities, analyze competencies, and research what is required. This book spells out in detail how to develop the plans, disciplines, and habits that will help you successfully accomplish your individual goals. No one can live your life for you; you make the choices. Some will be good, some will be bad. If you understand the choices you have and learn how to make well-thought-out, wise decisions, success is bound to follow.

Here are just a few of the guides and rules you will find in this book:

- 12 Habits of the Un-Lost
- 7 Ways to Turn Serendipity to Your Advantage
- 9 Ways Luck Can Find You
- 15 Areas in Which to Succeed
- 8 Steps to Recognizing if Your Dreams Can Become a Reality
- 6 Point Guide to Developing a Vision
- 8 Habits Needed to Make Your Vision Reality
- The 6 Stages of Life
- 8 Ways to Deal with Your Fears

- 8 Basic Questions to Ask When Planning
- 12 Trigger Questions to Help You See Yourself
- 7 Questions to Ask Yourself About Your Mission
- 10 Ways to Make Order Out of Chaos
- ABCs of Life
- 23 Habits of Success
- 7 Steps to Determine the Tools You Will Need
- 11 Keys to Gathering Information
- 11 Skills of a Good Networker
- 14 Places to Develop a Base for Contacts
- 10 Ways to Keep in Touch With Your Network
- 3 Ways to Set Your Budget for Living

The first section of the book is devoted to defining what I think success is and to help you to define what success will be for you. I also tell you how I went from feeling lost and hopeless to finding myself and the path to success. Luck and serendipity play a strong role in each of our lives. How you deal with what you can't control and how to take advantage of luck and serendipity are explored in detail. Your dreams and visions are also discussed. Guides and rules for turning your dreams or visions into reality are spelled out.

The second section is devoted to planning. In my view, planning is the major key to success. Finding yourself, knowing what you want out of life, and having a vision or dream of your future is the foundation upon which you build toward success. But the plan is the foundation upon which you actually construct success. You need to know how to develop a clear vision, a mission, goals, and strategies in order to achieve what you want in life. There are guides and work forms to help you do this and to show you how to develop a winning plan for yourself.

In the third section of the book, I deal with getting inside yourself so that you know what you're feeling and how to relate what you feel to the actions you take. Logic is one thing, your gut feelings are another. You must bring them into sync if you are to feel successful. You must also relate what you feel to what you plan in order to develop the drive and energy necessary for success. In this section, you will find discussions about new ways of seeing, of breaking paradigms, of discovering opportunities on the edge of chaos, how to obtain help from others, and how to form new habits that lead to success.

Section four deals with how much you want to earn in five, ten, or twenty years from now and how to determine which tools you will need to achieve these earnings. We also examine how to tailor these tools to your specific success criteria. Some of the tools include how to network, the best way to research, and

how to budget your resources—dollars, time, and
energy. Knowing and meeting your competition is
another factor. Whether we like it or not, the world
is competitive. Even those of you who may want to
find cooperative situations upon which to build your
life will surely have some competition. How you
face competition, your attitude toward it, and what
you do to meet competition are most important to
your success. There is also a time to take action, a
time to plan, and a time when you must act. Knowing
when to do what is explored.

Because the sentiment in the last paragraph of this
book is dear to me, I repeat it here.

I expect that most of the readers of this book will
be people much younger than I and I imagine there
will also be a few readers of my generation who seek
to change their lives and, therefore, will also find this
book of value. Whether you are the younger reader
or my contemporary, we all think about the years
ahead and about what to do with the rest of our lives.
*My prayer is that you will be granted years of health so that
you can work your plan, achieve your goals, and find joy
and happiness in the life you choose for yourself.*

—Ed Bobrow

Part I

Don't Spend Your Life Hiding Under a Blanket

Determine what success will be for you, find it within yourself, and set yourself on the right path.

1

WHEN YOU'RE LOST, SERENDIPITY HELPS

"Young man, the secret of my success is that at an early age I discovered I was not God."

—Oliver Wendell Holmes, Jr. in a reply to a reporter's question on his ninetieth birthday (March 8, 1931)

It was Christmas 1957. I was twenty-eight years old and had just lost my job—a job I did not like in a company I wasn't happy working for. Nevertheless, with a wife, an infant son, and no cash reserves, I could ill-afford to be out of work. I was unprepared. Sound familiar? Before I tell you what happened when I lost that job, let me give you a little background.

WHERE I CAME FROM

When I graduated from college in 1949, after having served in the army, I was in a very fortunate position. As I was still living at home, room and board were not an expense. For six months I worked for my Dad's Housewares Sales Agency. Then a neighbor offered me a position as advertising manager for the company he was with, Dr. Posner Shoes, manufacturers of children's shoes. Within a short time I was making $10,000 a year, an extremely well-paid position at that time, especially for a young man of twenty-four. I worked my way up to assistant to the president, Herbert Posner.

Although I was doing well and the people I worked with were great, and although I was learning more and more about how business operates, I decided I had to have my own business. I gave little thought to how I would do it—I just felt strongly that I wanted to be my own boss. With no cash reserves, still living in my parents' home, and still single, I thought I was already a success. After all, I was earning good money and had moved up in the corporate world. Why shouldn't it be easy to build my own business? Not so easy, as I discovered!

STARTING MY FIRST BUSINESS

I started Bobrow Sales Co., an independent sales rep agency selling to the automotive aftermarket. My executive assistant at Dr. Posner Shoes, Gloria Lefkowitz, helped me out in the evenings with some of the detail work. We had been friends at work but, in this new situation, we soon realized our attraction for each other. This resulted in shared hours of work and long conversations over dinner. We married a year later and have had a forty-five-year ongoing love affair.

About a year after I founded Bobrow Sales Co., my Dad started a new business and persuaded me to join him. I became a partner. A childhood dream of mine had been to someday work with my Dad; however, it did not work out. When I left, I took a job as advertising manager with Sunset Appliances. Within six months, merchandising manager was added to my duties, but without the power and authority to do the job—an unhappy situation for me. Perhaps one you yourself have experienced.

Sunset Appliances was the company that fired me at Christmastime without any severance pay. I remember one of the owners saying, "You will thank me for this one day," but I certainly felt no gratitude when he let me go.

I CRIED FOR DAYS

When I was fired, I realized my biggest problem was that I didn't know what I really wanted to do with my life. Have you ever had that feeling? Of course you have. I think it comes to almost everyone at some stage. All I knew was that I wanted to find work

I liked, make big money, be happy, and, if possible, be in business for myself—all glittering generalities.

I made the rounds of employment agencies. They all informed me that I had been earning too much money for my age and that the only jobs I could hope to get would be for a lot less money than what I was accustomed to earning. To bring in some much-needed income while job hunting, I sold advertising space, worked in a shoe store, and did almost anything to put bread on the table. I became depressed. I can say that now, but at the time was too macho to recognize it. One morning, under the blanket, not wanting to get out of bed, I cried. It took days to get hold of myself and begin to think of what I should do and where I could reach out for help.

I thought of my favorite uncle, Sam, who might be able to help me and I told him of my dilemma. After asking me a lot of questions, he agreed to help. Uncle Sam was able to get me a job interview for a sales manager's position with a paintbrush manufacturer, Masterset Paint Brushes. They were looking for someone with my energy and I was fortunate to get the job. The partner I worked for, Joe Schick, was a good guy. He did all he could to give me an opportunity and to teach me.

Within a year, however, I again became unhappy and knew for sure that I just had to be my own boss. I talked it over with Joe and Uncle Sam. They both agreed to help me get started in my own independent sales rep business, this time in the hardware field. It was one of the few businesses we could think of that I could get into with little or no capital. So, that's what I did. My first line was Masterset Paint Brushes. From the moment I made that decision I was a new person. I didn't know where the money would come from or how I would grow the business, but I was determined to succeed.

Now, I know you may not all have an Uncle Sam or a boss who is interested in you, but you can reach out to someone you know to find and develop a relationship with a mentor. Most importantly, you can find some relationships that will lead to what you want so that you can begin to make it happen. If you think you can't, this book will be your aid and comforter.

LESSONS I LEARNED

It has been said that we must learn from history (our own past) or we are doomed to repeat our mistakes. If we can't learn from the younger person that we were, then we will never be able to change and grow. Ask what you learned from yourself in the past in order to change the future. Here is what I learned:

- If you do what you don't enjoy, even though you may be good at it, you will not be happy nor will you optimize your abilities.

- Wishing will not make it so.

- I only knew what I wanted, but hadn't planned how to get it.

- I had done no networking and did not initially reach out for help.

- Hiding and/or crying may release tension, but solves nothing.

- Taking action often chases away depressed feelings.

- The owner of Sunset Appliances was right. Eventually I would thank him, for I learned that every ending is an opportunity for a new beginning.

- I found I needed specific goals. Glittering generalities are not actionable in and of themselves.

- Luck sure helps, but is no substitute for action.

TWELVE WAYS TO TELL IF YOU'RE HIDING

There is "hiding" and there is *hiding*. Sometimes you know why you are hiding and what you are hiding from. But often you *don't know* why you're hiding or what you're hiding from. Or you might be hiding when you don't even know you're hiding. Whichever hiding you might be doing, the bottom line is that you are trying to escape a reality that you don't like and find difficult to live with. Although the young person that I was knew why he was hiding from the world and from himself, there were times when he *didn't know* why he was hiding, just as there will be times when you won't know. You can usually tell if you're hiding if you experience any of these symptoms:

1. Most of the time you have an anxious feeling in the pit of your stomach.

2. Your heart races for no apparent reason.

3. You feel as if there are ten tons of weight on your head.

4. You have trouble sleeping.

5. You only want to sleep.

6. You experience an unusual amount of anger.

7. You yell at someone and later realize that it really wasn't them you were yelling at, it's just that they were a convenient and safe outlet.

8. Everything is everybody's fault but yours.

9. You overeat.

10. You lose your appetite.

11. You drink too much.

12. You have to do drugs.

What Do You Do When You Feel Lost?

Everyone has a different way of coping with that "lost" feeling. Some seek professional help. Others try relaxation techniques: Yoga, exercise, meditation, biofeedback, Tai Chi, deep breathing, imaging, screaming into a pillow, any of a myriad of tension- and anxiety-releasing techniques. I have tried most of them over the years and found that they all have some value and often give immediate release, which enables you to take action. But none solve the problem of being lost. They may open you up to act, but until you can get yourself into directed action, you will not eliminate that lost feeling.

Sometimes we get stuck being lost and can't envision anything but despair. That's when professional help may be needed. When the young me was hiding, I thought nothing would get me out of it. It took love and understanding from my wife, attention from my little son, and, most of all, sheer will to get myself back into their world. Once I got out from under the covers and involved in their daily lives again, I was able to start exercising and take long contemplative walks. This led me to think about how bad things were and how much I wanted circumstances to be different. It was the nexus of where I was and where I wanted to be that brought me to the realization that no matter how much support one gets from family and friends, we are indeed, as Lily

Tomlin said, "All in this alone." It was up to me to help me. I also realized that if I was going to achieve what I envisioned my life to be, I had to plan for it to happen.

TWELVE HABITS OF THE UN-LOST

The un-lost know what they want and usually are working to get it. Obvious, right! And true. If they didn't know what they wanted, they would be lost. It is no surprise, however, to find that even the un-lost become lost at times. If you aren't lost now and think you never will be, you're wrong. It's a good bet that during one or more stages or ages in your life you will feel lost.

As you read along in this book you will learn, as I have, what to do when you inevitably hit a period of feeling lost. But, for now, here are the key habits of people who have been un-lost for most of their lives. They have:

1. a dream or vision of their lives.

2. articulated or unarticulated goals.

3. trained themselves to focus.

4. the ability to concentrate on what is at hand.

5. discipline.

6. passion for what they do and for life.

7. high curiosity.

8. plans for what they want to achieve.

9. become action-oriented.

10. reached out to people and establish networks.

11. the courage to follow their convictions.

12. stick-to-itiveness.

YOU NEED A PLAN

Directed action begins by envisioning and fantasizing what you would like your life to be. If you can't envision or dream it, you won't be able to plan and work toward your deep-down wants and needs; or, as Casey Stengel, the baseball immortal, said, "If you don't know where you're going, you might wind up somewhere else." I remember my young self taking a sheet of paper and beginning a list of goals. His first goal was to establish his own business. What would be your first goal? Would it be to get a job, change jobs, join a particular profession, obtain more schooling, be married, have children, make a lot of money (what is a lot for you?), be happy (what does happy mean to you?)…what? You have to start somewhere to direct your life. What better way than to envision the future you would like and spell it out in goals.

If you choose to go through life rudderless, without planning, you are usually powerless. If you want to be able to choose where you will go with your life and how you will get there, you need clear goals and strategies. Only then will you have the power to direct your life and to marshal your personal resources productively. Whether you are aware of your goals and strategies or not, they are steering your life. But when you bring them into full consciousness, through planning, you become the captain who steers your life successfully. Just remember: *Those who choose to go through life rudderless are usually powerless.* Don't be a powerless person. Take charge of your life today. Read on for how to do it.

SERENDIPITY HELPS

Webster's *Ninth Collegiate Dictionary* offers these definitions:

Serendipity: the faculty of finding valuable or agreeable things not sought for

Luck: (a) force that brings good fortune or adversity (b) events or circumstances that operate for or against an individual (c) to prosper or succeed especially through chance or good fortune

Near the end of World War II, at age seventeen, I enlisted in the Army Specialized Training Program. I was sent to Clemson University, at that time a military college, to study engineering. Luckily for me, after about six months, they closed down the program.

I say luckily because I was not doing well scholastically, although physically I was in the best shape of my young life.

After a short time I was ordered to Aberdeen Proving Grounds, Ordnance Corps, for basic training. They had asked where I would like to be assigned. The army being what it is, they did not honor my request but sent me where they wanted. When I completed my basic training I was sent to a Holding Company to await orders for assignment. While at the Holding Company you usually did KP duty (kitchen police), garbage detail, guard duty, or any other distasteful task that needed doing. Here is the serendipitous thing that happened to me just before moving to the Holding Company.

SERENDIPITY AT PLAY

While waiting my turn for a haircut at the base barbershop, I talked with a soldier sitting next to me. He and I were both from New York. We exchanged pleasantries and information about what companies we were in and the jobs we held. We were both surprised to find that I was moving into the Holding Company that he would be moving out of. I was to move the next day and he was to ship out the day after that. He told me he was on permanent Night CQ (Charge of Quarters) duty, the best job you could get in a Holding Company because you worked at Company Headquarters from four in the afternoon until midnight with no other duty and had a class A pass for the rest of the time. Sure enough, when I arrived at the Holding Company, there he was. He introduced me to the Master Sergeant in charge and, after a brief interview, I was told to start the next day. Serendipity at work!

A STROKE OF LUCK

While on duty as Permanent Night CQ, one of the soldiers returned dead drunk about ten minutes after his pass expired. He literally passed out in the office. I had a choice—follow the letter of the regulations and report him on two counts and call the MPs (Military Police) or get him safely to his barracks and to bed. Being in good physical shape, I was able to lift him, put him over my shoulder, and carry him to his barracks and to his bed. I took off his shoes, opened his collar, and covered him. Here is where I got lucky.

The next day his buddies told him what had happened. He came into the office that evening to thank me. We talked for a while and I warned him that if the sergeant had been around I would not have been able to cover for him. He promised it wouldn't happen again. As we spoke, I learned that he was one of the clerks who cut orders for assignment out of the Holding Companies. A week or so later he stopped by again and told me that my name had come up to have my orders cut for a new assignment and that he had held it up until he could talk with me. He gave me several choices of assignment. One was a particularly good assignment with a motor pool at Fort

Jackson, South Carolina, where there was just one opening. If he had not intervened, I would have been shipped to Alaska where most of the others were being sent. It was good luck for me, brought about through a serendipitous convergence of events.

SEVEN WAYS TO TURN SERENDIPITY TO YOUR ADVANTAGE

What did I learn from that soldier? Whatever I did learn, I sure didn't learn it at the moment it happened. After several other serendipitous events, I came to realize that while you can't create them, you sure can take advantage of them. Here is how you can turn serendipity to your advantage:

1. Be constantly on the alert to what is happening to you and around you. Learn to recognize when a situation is a serendipitous opportunity.

2. Engage people in conversation at chance meetings. If I had read a magazine at the barber shop or had spoken only a few words with the fellow next to me, I never would have known that we were both from New York, which then led to his providing me with the lucky opportunity to become Permanent Night CQ.

3. Ask people you meet questions about themselves. Not prying questions, but questions that show genuine interest. People love to talk about themselves. Don't you?

4. Look around you and see what's going on.

5. Know what your goals are so that when an incident does happen, you can use that incident to help you achieve your goals.

6. Build a network of contacts and develop a card index or, better still, a database. You never know when you might have something that will help another person or when you might want to reach out for someone's help.

LUCK CAN STRIKE AT ANY TIME

Gloria and I had been married almost fourteen years when we decided that we could finally afford a larger apartment, one outside the area where we had always lived. We had read an article in the *New York Times* about an unusual building that was being built along the Hudson River in the Riverdale section of the Bronx. We visited the site, dreaming that someday we might be able to afford to live there. The architecture of the building was unusual. It sat above the greenbelt along the Hudson River. It had large spacious rooms, a great view of the Hudson, a fireplace, a terrace facing the river, tennis courts, an outdoor swimming pool, and plenty of trees and greenery.

We loved the style of the building, its setting, and the layout of the rooms. We did a careful analysis of our financial situation and finally, with great trepidation, decided we could chance the new costs that moving to that building would bring. We were so nervous when we signed the lease that we almost backed out. Well, renting that apartment turned out to be one of the best things we ever did. Our finances improved and we and our son were very comfortable there for some years. Then, one day, the owner decided that he was going to turn the building into a condominium and cash out his investment.

Lucky for Us

We were very worried when the owner decided to convert the building to a condominium. There were many tenant meetings. People wondered how they could ever afford to buy an apartment, whether it would be a good buy, and how the condo would fare under tenant management. Luckily for us, the owner came up with a great plan that included an excellent price, low down payment, and low interest rates on the mortgage. He had arranged a very attractive package that was difficult to refuse. Even though it meant a financial stretch at that time, we bought the apartment. Through the trials of learning how to live and manage the building as owners, we finally reached a point where it was efficiently and happily run.

Then we really got lucky! After living in the building for twenty-two years, we decided it was time for a change. Our son was an adult with his own apartment and we wanted to move into Manhattan. We found a lovely smaller apartment suitable for my wife and me. Coincidentally, it just happened to be a sellers' market. Would you believe that we were able to get ten times what we had paid for the Riverdale apartment? It wasn't that we were smart or that we calculated that this would happen. It was sheer luck that the market was up when we were ready for a change and up to such a degree. After we moved into our new home, we had more good luck. On the same floor of the building where we bought our coop, we met a wonderful couple with whom we became very close friends. In this vast city, what are the odds of finding another couple close by that you have much in common with? Once again, luck.

NINE WAYS LUCK CAN FIND YOU

Here are some ways to prepare yourself to take advantage of luck when it crosses your path:

1. Be prepared to take advantage of whatever may come along, good or bad. If we had not been putting away some savings, we never could have made the down payment on a condo. If, unfortunately, an illness had come along instead of an opportunity to

own our home, our savings would have helped us there as well.

2. Take a thorough look at whatever opportunity presents itself. You never know which ones may prove to be the good luck opportunities.

3. Have plans so that when a situation arises you will know whether it fits into your plan.

4. Train yourself to be an analytical thinker.

5. Don't hide under a blanket. Instead, put yourself in places where opportunities can develop.

6. Be out there. Luck is not likely to strike if you sit at home.

7. Work your contacts and network, network, network.

8. Develop a database of contacts. Keep in touch with your contacts. Let them know what's going on in your life and find out what's happening in theirs.

9. Get involved. Don't be a bystander. Right from the beginning, when our Riverdale apartment became a condominium, I made sure I was on the Board during the transition time and involved in the planning and running of the building. I put myself on the

front line so that I would have the best possible information and firsthand knowledge of the affairs of the building.

Don't Just Sit There—Do Something!

If you think some great serendipitous thing will happen to you or that you will have good luck by just sitting around and waiting—you're wrong. As the characters in the play *Waiting for Godot* by Samuel Beckett discovered: You can wait and wait, and wish and wish, and talk and talk your whole life through, but no one will come along and suddenly make everything all right.

There is another reason not to sit around and wait. There is a direct relationship between how hard you work and going after what you want, and good luck catching up to you. I don't know of anyone who had observations, thoughts, dreams, and desires—but didn't act on them—who became successful. Let me emphasize: don't sit and wait. Establish some goals, get into action, and, while being active, something good may come your way.

2

What Is Success and Do You Really Want It?

When I no longer felt lost, I kept asking myself: What would success be for me? Back in the fifties, I thought that if I could earn $25,000 a year I would be a success. I thought that if I could accumulate a million dollars, I would be on top of the world. When I did accomplish these goals, I felt no more successful than I did prior to their achievement.

When I started my own business with my brother-in-law in 1956, I asked my Dad for advice. We talked about how to get started, where to get help, and, most important, the impact it would have on my life. The conversation took a turn toward "becoming a success." My Dad told me it wouldn't be easy but, if I were successful, it would all be worthwhile. Dad then asked what success meant to me. My immediate answer was a dollar amount. Dad was wise enough to counsel that success was not only about money but that there were many other areas to consider in becoming a success—feeling happy; enjoying my work; being a good husband and father; becoming an active member of the community. He emphasized that it was most important to feel happy and fulfilled in one's life and one's work in order to be truly successful.

After that conversation, I began to rethink success. Over the years I have often asked myself the question, "Am I successful?" The answer varied, depending on what was going on in my life at the time. I came to realize success is not a fixed point and certainly not universally perceived; it is individual and changes as we grow and experience the world. It is a changing target that you spend your life pursuing, not a point that you finally arrive at.

There have been many times, and I hope there will be many in your life, when I have felt successful. Sometimes it was when my peers gave me recognition. Other times it was knowing I had reached a certain level of economic security. Too often it was overcoming health problems. At other times it was having a book published that was well-received by its target audience. As my very wise old Uncle Iz said to me—after my first book was published and I asked him why there was no big bang at seeing it in print— "It's all in the doing." He was right! The satisfaction is in the journey, not in the destination.

ONE PERSON'S SUCCESS IS ANOTHER'S FAILURE

"I look at what I have not and think myself to be unhappy; others look at what I have and think me to be happy."

—Manufacturers Agents Association's newsletter, *MANA Matters,* First Quarter of 1998, anonymous

"Look at all the money she's made! What a success! Wow, is she famous!" "Did you see him on television? That guy I went to school with seems to have everything! Did you see the Rolls Royce he's driving? You know he wrote a book and it's in all the bookstores. What a success he must be!"

To the world, people like this are often labeled a success. But the big question is—do they themselves feel they are a success? How satisfied are they with their lives; are they happy with what they are doing and what they have achieved; is there anything intruding in their lives to overshadow the feeling of success; are they, in fact, realizing their dreams?

MANY KINDS OF SUCCESS

The outward signs of success—usually material success—often label a person a success. People who are renowned or famous are also considered successful but may have lives that are falling apart, may not have achieved what they set out to do, or don't perceive themselves a success and, therefore, don't feel that they are successful. *It is only when you have an inner feeling of success, because you have achieved what you set out to do, that you are truly successful.* This inner feeling of success is the most valuable as it is based on the achievement of your vision of success, not on someone else's. What you see as success may not be what I see as success. You must be very sure you know what you mean when you say "I want to be a success." Here are some different kinds of success:

Monetary: You have a lot of money. What one person thinks is a lot may not be for another. Someone with a million dollars seems to be a success, but may not be thought successful by the person with tens of millions of dollars. The multimillionaire may not be thought of as a success by the billionaire. To the outside world, monetary success is relative to what your financial position is to others. Monetary success for you occurs when you achieve your financial goals.

Image: Some people portray the image of success. They drive big cars, dress well, and exude an aura of success. They may, however, be in debt or on the verge of bankruptcy. They may have achieved nothing of substance or are trying to build their image so they can become as successful in their own eyes as they seem to be to the world. It's the old philosophy:

Look successful, act successful, and you will become successful.

Fame: Some people think success is twenty minutes of being in the public eye. To others, it is peer recognition. We tend to think of famous public figures as successful because we see or hear about them often—actors, models, sports figures, politicians, and others in the public eye. Certainly Mike Tyson is famous. He was a success as a boxer when he was a champion, but is he now truly a success or just famous?

Overcoming adversity: People who overcome adversity—an illness, an addiction, the loss of a loved one, or any of the other terrible things life deals out—are certainly deemed successful for surviving their pain and misery. To the world, they may seem ordinary. To those who understand their plight, they are heroes, successful at handling adversity.

Peer success: This kind of success occurs when you are successful and are recognized by the people within your field of activity.

Achieving your goals: The best inner success is to achieve your dreams and your goals. Dreams turned into specific goals are the measure you can use to determine if you are indeed successful unto yourself. It may or may not be what the outside world sees as success, but it is what your inner self knows to be success.

Most of us want more than one kind of success. We want recognition among our peers; we want money; some of us want fame; others may want to be successful in overcoming an adversity. But we all want some recognition for what we are doing with our lives.

WHAT WILL SUCCESS BE FOR YOU?

Often we think that one person or another has a perfect life. Mary Tyler Moore was a smash hit on television. She had a long run on the Dick Van Dyke Show, acted in movies and the theater, and had her own long and successful TV show. She is beautiful, famous, talented, and rich, but she has had as tough a life as many of us. Does that mean she is or is not successful?

Ms. Moore, it is reported, was an alcoholic, lost a son, suffered from diabetes and cancer, was divorced several times, suffered from depression, and all in all had it pretty tough over the years. Was she a success? Certainly her long-running show was a commercial, popular, and critical success. She has received award after award validating her success. However, that does not mean she herself feels she is a success. We don't know what she feels. But if she has achieved her goals, then she certainly is a success unto herself.

Our feelings about success change at different periods in our lives. One day you're up, feeling great, puffing up your chest and thinking, "how great I am." Another day you're down, feeling miserable and a failure. *How you feel about yourself is the true measure of success.* You may have a financially successful business or career and others may see you as successful, but it is only when you have achieved the goals that you have set for yourself that you are truly successful unto yourself. This is why one person's success may not be success for another.

The key is to determine what success is for you. Saying, "I just want to be happy," defines nothing. You have to figure out what it is that makes you happy and then pursue it. Is it money, fame, achieving goals, overcoming diversity, achieving within a given field, or a combination of these and other things?

> *"The moral flabbiness born of the exclusive worship of the bitch-goddess SUCCESS. That—with the squalid cash interpretation put on the word success—is our national disease."*

—William James, 1942–1910. *The Letters of William James* (1920). To H.G. Wells, September 11, 1906 (William Barclay, 1976)

FIFTEEN AREAS FOR SUCCESS AND STILL COUNTING

When you think of success, think about the various areas in your life in which you want to achieve success. Some possibilities are listed below. This is my list and may coincide with yours. Add to or subtract

from these fifteen areas to build your own list. Then
define what your success will be for each of the specific areas.

1. money

2. work

3. politics

4. school

5. religion

6. health

7. happiness

8. marriage

9. children

10. hobbies

11. sports

12. family

13. community

14. charities

15. scholarship

To define what success is for you takes a good deal
of thought. For this exercise to be most effective,
write down your definitions. In the future, you can
look back at the milestones for success you set for

yourself. For example, you may think you will feel successful if you become president of a charitable organization. You will feel the blush of success when you achieve it. I would bet, however, that once you have become president, you will find your idea of success shifts to the agenda you have set for the organization. When you reach those objectives, you will again feel the blush of success. The point is that success is a moving target that, once achieved, needs new goals and accomplishments in order to satisfy the continuing desire for success. It is not a point at which you arrive and say, "Wow, I'm a success; now I can rest on my laurels."

Only when you know what success will be for you will you know when you have arrived there.

NOW YOU'VE GOT IT— OR HAVE YOU?

Well, I sure don't know if you really have got it or not. Only you know that. But if you are beginning to look at success differently, then you are on your way.

Success is not just making money, getting a better job, or achieving a certain rank in life; rather it is a composite of all areas of your life. For some the only measure may be money. If you are one of those people, I think you are kidding yourself. Money is certainly a great measure to the outside world, like fame and celebrity; these successes are more public than personal. Unless you know what a famous person thinks and feels about what she has achieved or what the billionaire thinks success is for him, you don't know if they are successful within themselves.

Money was never a driving force for me. Yes, I wanted money, but as a young man I was more into doing my own thing and obtaining recognition and respect within my work environment. I wanted to do what I enjoyed doing. That desire drove me more than anything else. When my wife and I took our first vacation not associated with business, some twenty-odd years after starting our company, it felt like work to me. When I was at work, however, it felt as if I were on vacation because I really loved what I was doing. It certainly is a form of success to feel that way about the work you do and spend most of the waking hours of the day doing it.

I didn't begin to take charge of my life, however, until I felt like a failure. At that low point, when I was hiding, I began to analyze what I wanted out of life. I had to know my destination if I was ever going to get there, let alone be a success. So do you.

To evaluate success you must look at how the world perceives you and then at how you perceive yourself—externally to the world and internally to yourself. Some people believe that how the world sees them is of utmost importance. They measure everything about themselves in terms of other people.

To others, and I hope to you, how they see themselves is of prime importance. We all want the world to accept us and to think well of us. First and foremost, however, we must see ourselves as successful if we want to be a success.

UNDERSTANDING YOUR NEEDS LEADS TO SUCCESS

We all have gratification needs. To understand these needs may help us understand our inner needs for success. Let's look at them and use them as a guide toward understanding where we're coming from in our search for success.

Abraham Maslow, the father of the humanistic school of psychology, established a theory of the hierarchy of needs. It was his contention that mankind has five levels of needs. Here they are listed from the most basic to the most creative.

1. **Physiological:** the basic needs, such as hunger, thirst, shelter, clothing, reproduction

2. **Safety/Security:** stability, law and order, pensions, and the need for structure

3. **Love/Belonging:** belonging, gaining acceptance, looking for love

4. **Self-esteem:** gaining respect, recognition, attention, a feeling of importance

5. **Self-actualization:** creative expression, full self-expression, challenge

Maslow contended that a person moves from one level of needs to another. Once the lower level needs are satisfied, higher order needs develop; the lowest order of needs are the physiological and the highest are self-actualization needs. Although people move up and down this hierarchy, they tend to concentrate on certain levels. Some people are oriented toward security and safety, others to belonging and love, and other people to another level. The diagram at right illustrates the levels.

Throughout our lives we move up and down the hierarchy, depending on what is happening to us at the time and what stage of life we are in. When I first went into business, I needed to sustain my physiological needs. As they were taken care of, I started to acquire things, to protect what I had, and to provide protection for my family. Once those needs were taken care of, I became more interested in acceptance, recognition, and self-esteem. Finally, as I became more successful, from my own viewpoint, I was able to become more self-actualized, to exercise creativity, and to take charge of my own destiny. In most of my life today, I am a self-actualized person. I need to create to satisfy my inner needs—it is the reason I write. When I produce an article or a book that receives acclaim, I feel successful. If I were strongly

**SELF-
ACTUALIZATION
Needs:
Self-fulfillment,
Opportunity to become
what you can become,
Creative expression**

**SELF-ESTEEM
Needs:
Recognition, Status, Appreciation, Respect**

**BELONGING, LOVE
Needs:
To love and to be loved, To be accepted, Affection**

**SECURITY, SAFETY
Needs:
Order, Discipline, Protection, Material Acquisitions**

**PHYSIOLOGICAL
Needs:
Food, Water, Shelter**

Maslow's Hierarchy of Needs

concerned with self-esteem, I would probably have tried to become a more public person, although I do seek recognition in my work.

Knowing what drives you will help you determine the areas within yourself on which to concentrate in your pursuit of inner success.

As it is possible to move up and down the hierarchy, the level you are in at any particular stage in your life does not make you less of a person than someone who may be higher up the hierarchy. You can, so to speak, fall off the triangle. Even though you may be self-actualized now, it is possible, later in life, to become much more safety and security oriented. I find at this stage in my life that security keeps pulling at me. I don't take the risks that I used to take, and though I still have a need to create, I am not self-actualized at the price of safety and security.

To become aware of your true self, how you feel and how you act will help you to be realistic in setting your vision. Give a lot of thought to where you fit on Maslow's hierarchy. Ask your closest friends where they think you fit. Do they agree with what you think? If not, consider whether you are fooling yourself or if your friends do not know you as well as you thought. Resolve the differences, then relate your conclusion to the vision of the future you have for yourself. Do they match?

It All Starts with a Dream

The first step on the road to success is to be able to imagine what you want to successfully accomplish—dream it, envision it, hold a vision of it. Can you possibly imagine doing something big and important without dreaming of it first? Dream of owning your own house, buying a certain kind of car, starting your own business, getting a masters or doctoral degree, becoming a doctor or lawyer, or whatever else you can think of.

Vision is a mode of seeing, conceiving, or having foresight.

Once you have the dream or vision of what you want to achieve, you can set goals and strategies to accomplish it. We will talk about goals and strategies later in the book.

Eight Steps to Recognizing Whether Your Dreams Can Become Reality

All dreams cannot become reality. Here is a guide to help you recognize those that can.

1. The first step: put your dream into words. Describe what you envision your future to be and what you are willing to commit yourself to.

2. It is one thing to daydream about being a sports figure like Michael Jordan, a great actor like Vanessa Redgrave, or a leader, a writer, or whatever you may dream of. In order for your dream to become reality you must have the talent and commitment to make it come true. Although it often seems that someone has become a success overnight, it seldom happens that way. It takes years of preparation, practice, and commitment to build your dream, usually one step at a time.

3. Make a list of why you want the vision to become a reality. Your list should tell you whether the reasons are real or pipe dreams and if the reasons really meet your inner needs.

4. Make another list of what it will take to make it happen: years of schooling, an apprenticeship, contact building, whatever will be necessary. Are you truly willing to commit to the long hard road? What is really required to become a great lawyer, doctor, businessperson, or whatever you dream of becoming?

5. Is your vision what you think it is? If you envision a particular thing but have no realistic knowledge of what it involves each

day of your life to achieve it, you won't know if the price is worth paying. You need to find out what a person must do, day in and day out, to achieve that vision. Don't forget, we see the fame and the fortune of others, but not the work, sweat, or tears expended to get there.

6. Would you enjoy the kind of work it takes to get there? We often have a glamorized ideal of others' success. We only put ourselves in their shoes after they have received the rewards, recognition, or fame, but not when they walked the walk, mile after difficult mile.

7. Does what you have to do to attain your vision meet your values and philosophy? I know that I could have made a lot more money and gotten much more recognition than I have, but the things I would have had to do on that road would have gone against my values and my philosophy of doing business. I therefore opted for less money and recognition, but never compromised my values or my philosophy.

8. How will the path necessary for you to take relate to the various people in your life? Is it compatible with family and loved ones?

Remember, it takes not just the head, but the heart and soul to make the journey.

A Six-Point Guide for Developing a Vision

Dreams have to be converted into active visions. Here is a guide for doing just that.

1. Examine where you have been and where you are now in relation to your vision. As life moves on, visions change. If you don't know where you have been, where you are now, or where you are going, it will be difficult to find the right road to travel.

2. Do you really want the vision you have or is it just something nice to dream about?

3. Convert the dream into a written statement. You *must* write it down. If you just plan and think in your mind, it will slip into daydreaming. When you write your dream down, it brings a sense of reality to your thoughts.

4. Don't be afraid to act on your intuition. Logic is important, but the great leaps are made from intuitive insights that are then logically pursued.

5. Test the validity of your vision. Is it achievable or does it need to be adjusted or sublimated? Research is an important part of testing the reality. Look into everything involved, in detail, that is necessary to achieve your vision.

6. Carry your vision with you on paper at all times as a reminder of your dream. Look at your current actions to see how they relate to or will help you achieve your vision or dream.

TEN HABITS THAT WILL MAKE YOUR VISION A REALITY

Mark Twain said, *"Habit is habit, and is not to be flung out the window by any man, but coaxed downstairs a step at a time."*

Habits, as you well know, are hard to get rid of and even harder to acquire. I have always found that exploring habits in full consciousness is necessary in order to break bad habits or to take on new ones.

One device I have used successfully is to post notes of what I am trying to remember to do or not do in places where the actions related to the habit are most likely to occur. You may want to remind yourself of the habit you are trying to change or acquire when you wake up in the morning, or when writing things down, or while working at the computer, for example. Wherever the key places are that the habit is likely to manifest itself, I leave a note to do or not do such and such. I also keep my vision, goals, and strategies on one piece of paper and look at it every day.

The following habits are well-worth cultivating in order to be successful at anything you pursue.

1. Always exercise excellence.

2. Attend to the details, for that is where success lies.

3. Take pride in being creative, even if it means you are being different.

4. Think of how what you do today will influence achieving your dream tomorrow.

5. Develop a picture of the future and hold it in your mind and heart.

6. Think in terms of goals.

7. Monitor your progress.

8. Know what success will be for you.

9. Prepare, prepare, prepare.

10. Do it now.

When I give a workshop on a subject I am familiar with, it would be easy for me to use notes or slides from previous presentations or lectures. But I never do that. In my pursuit of the habit of excellence, I address the details and always prepare. First, I make sure I know who my audience will be. Then I build new notes for the level and interest of that group. New material that is of special interest to the group is added; then I review all the material to make sure it relates to the audience. I never wait until the last minute. No matter how many times I may present a particular subject, I do not want to rely on having to hastily prepare material at the last minute. I want to be sure I have sufficient time to do it thoughtfully and thoroughly.

It took time for me to learn and to develop these habits, and it has paid off. Early on in my career I had to remind myself over and over to do these things until they finally became habits. The notes I made on the books I used for my preparation proved to be constant reminders to always do the detail work, to prepare, and to do the best job I could. When I was tired or in a hurry, my notes reminded me that I must be constant if I was to achieve my vision of becoming a professional consultant. The habits are still with me today.

3

The Life Cycle of Success: Struggling with Your Comfort Zone

*"God grant you life until your work is done,
and work until your life is over."*

—Reverend Peter J. Gomes
Plummer Professor of Christian Morals, Harvard University

The day I turned 70, in the midst of writing this book, was the day in my life when I felt the most successful. My wife gave me a lovely birthday party attended by family, friends, and people I have mentored through the years. I experienced the most loving feeling I have ever received from a group of people. The birthday toasts made by my wife and son and remarks from others touched me deeply. Until then, the happiest days I had ever experienced were my wedding day, the day my son was born, and his wedding day. As wonderful as they were, I did not feel the same surge of success.

The afterglow and feeling of success felt on my seventieth birthday are still with me. I don't think I would have felt that way if I had had such a birthday party ten, twenty, or thirty years ago. I had to reach a certain stage in my life where former successes were behind me to be open to the full appreciation of the honor bestowed upon me. It brought home the knowledge that, whatever success is for each of us, it is different at various stages of our lives.

You're Not the Person at Fifty You Were at Twenty

At twenty, I certainly had not developed the kinds of relationships I had at seventy. Although I had friends and a loving family, success meant my grades at college and my next sexual conquest. The grades worked out fine, the conquests—sometimes. But I was focused on getting my college degree as quickly as possible so that I could start my business career. I felt I had already lost time in the army. A year later I completed school with a B+ grade average. I thought I knew it all and I was ready to test myself in business.

My first position was advertising manager with Dr. Posner Shoes, a company with the wisdom to know that I would learn from my mistakes—and I made plenty of them. I soon realized how much I didn't know and signed up for graduate school at New York University to pursue my Masters of Business Administration in the evening.

At that time I began to pay attention to my mistakes and ask: Why did I make that mistake? How could I have avoided this one? What did I do that was wrong in this situation? I discovered that I could learn more from my mistakes than from my successes, providing I analyzed the why, how, when, where, and what.

- Why did I make that mistake? Was it because it was the wrong thing to do, or was it in the doing itself? Often we undertake the wrong thing, and even though we may do it correctly, it still proves to be a mistake.

- How did the mistake come about? Looking at the history of what happened before and after the mistake will help you avoid the mistake in the future.

- Where did I go wrong? You must analyze mistakes, take them apart, examine them, and determine what you did right in the situation and what you did wrong.

- When we do the right thing wrong, it is usually because we lack experience, did not study the situation sufficiently, didn't pay attention to the details, or did not prepare properly before acting.

- What can I learn from this mistake?

You certainly will learn from your successes and goals achieved, but not as much as you will learn from your mistakes—if you don't run from them but, instead, give them close attention.

You never stay the same person you were as you march through life. You are always changing, growing, and learning from mistakes. As you engage in life, no matter what age you reach, you build upon the past to become the new person of the present.

KEEP CHECKING: WHO AM I NOW?

> *"The life which is unexamined*
> *is not worth living."*
>
> —Plato, *Dialogues,* "Apology"

I have found that at twenty or at fifty, or now at seventy, you must continue to learn from the person you were yesterday. You can only do this if you have a full understanding of who you are now. When you are young, you don't often think of how life will be as you become chronologically older. If, however, you start to think in terms of "Who I am now?" "Where have I been?" and "Where do I want to go?" you will begin to realize that you can exercise some control over your future, now.

WHO AM I NOW?

This involves an understanding of yourself. List the qualities you feel you possess under each of the following topics.

- List what you think motivates you. Go back to the last chapter and take another look at Maslow's hierarchy of needs.

- List your likes and dislikes.

- Make an honest list of your strengths and weaknesses.

- List how you will accomplish the next things you want—your goals.

WHERE HAVE I BEEN?

A clear understanding of where you have been— where you're coming from—is to know whether you have the background, talent, skill, competency, and ability to move ahead in a particular direction. Make a list for each of the following areas:

- Skills
- Talents

- Abilities
- Competencies

Then draw up a list of the skills, talents, abilities, and competencies you need to achieve your goals. Match them to the ones you already have. You will have a clear picture of what you still need to acquire.

WHERE DO I WANT TO GO?

Goals, goals, goals—I implore you to be clear about your goals. You have to know your hoped-for destination if you are to know the road and the vehicles to take in order to arrive at the destination of your dreams. Commit your goals to paper, too.

HOW WILL YOU GET THERE?

How you reach your goals is often called strategy, or the way you set out to accomplish your goals. List your strategies on paper.

These lists will help you analyze yourself, your goals, and what is required to achieve these goals. Part II describes planning in detail. I suggest devices to use and provide forms to help you plan for success.

THE SIX STAGES OF LIFE

As life is different for each of us, beware of generalizations. Having said that, I will make the generalization that we all go through the following stages as we move through the years.

Years of Wonder. These are the childhood years when we are free to play and to wonder. They are the years— usually from birth to five years old—before formal schooling, before we begin to acquire the discipline necessary to direct our lives. Feeling secure and loved is success for most of us during this stage.

Years of Discipline. Although we begin to learn discipline in the years of wonder, organized discipline starts with formal schooling at five years old and continues throughout our lives. Achievement in school becomes our main measure of success.

Adulthood. This is the stage in life when we become responsible for our own actions and their consequences. It is when we take charge of our disciplines and habits and become totally responsible for our actions. This usually starts around age fourteen or fifteen. Success takes on many individual guises, from school activities to social, religious, spiritual, work, community, and other activities.

Experienced Adulthood. This stage includes the years after formal schooling when we gain life experiences. It generally starts whenever formal schooling ends, but most often starts with our first employment when the realities of life kick in. Success then becomes: satisfying our inner needs, meeting our goals, accumulating money, gaining recognition—all the myriad things we need to feel successful during this time.

Mature Age. This stage occurs when we have experienced much of life and have won or lost our battles for success. The success that becomes important is to love and be loved, security, recognition, and whatever else that gives us the inner satisfaction of a life well spent.

Old Age. This stage can occur when we have given up doing and just exist. Success is never letting ourselves fall into this stage, if we can help it, no matter what chronological age we reach.

THERE WILL BE UPS AND DOWNS

As we go through these life stages, success takes on a different meaning. After college, I thought that if I could get a good job, drive a big car, and have fun, I would be a success. Although I quickly achieved all these goals, I did not feel like a success. I began to realize that there was a deeper need within me to find other areas in my life that would have more meaning. My goals for success changed. I wanted to learn as much as possible, but I also wanted to do as much as possible to achieve business success. I took on any opportunity my job presented. When I offered to write a book about children's shoes, Mr. Posner, president of the company, asked, "Is there anything you won't undertake?" I became the spokesman (we didn't have spokeswomen or a spokesperson in those days) for the company and, at twenty-four, appeared on some of what were then the most popular radio and television talk shows. I began to think I was really a big shot and a great success. I was also responsible for the company's TV show, *Six Gun Playhouse*, and helped develop other formats for the company's TV effort when it became necessary to change the show's format.

I met celebrities and a few very famous people. One of my greatest experiences was the day I worked with Mrs. Eleanor Roosevelt on a TV show we put together celebrating United Nations Children's Day. To work with her and the children was inspiring and educational. I saw how a truly great and successful person interacts with other people. She was kind and gentle, patient, and never spoke down to any of us. Her worldly success and fame did not have to be on display.

While working on the television shows, I realized that it takes a team effort to have a successful show. Our advertising agency, production people, and many others were integral in making it happen. I always made sure they received credit. And when things didn't go as planned, I took full responsibility.

I paid close attention to why we failed so it wouldn't happen again, then I attempted to build a success on the failure.

WHAT TO EXPECT AS LIFE MOVES ON

Not everyone can be an Edison, an Eleanor Roosevelt, a Bill Gates, a Lincoln, a Shakespeare, or any of the exceptionally talented people the world produces. I learned quickly enough as I moved into "experienced adulthood" that I did not have a special talent or the ability to be in a league with the truly great. Oh, I used to dream of being great, but I knew deep down that it was wishful thinking and would only produce nice daydreams or great discontent. I did not let those daydreams get in the way of addressing what my actual abilities were and what I could and could not do. Thereafter, I devoted myself to planning how to accomplish as much as I could.

You can expect many failures and successes as you move through life. There will be ups and downs, dreams realized and dreams lost. It takes time to learn to accept what cannot be changed and to steadfastly go after the goals that can be realized. Be realistic. Appraise your talents and abilities, work toward optimizing them, and use them to achieve your vision of life.

To find your comfort zone is to be able to find that balance in your life where you have more periods of being centered than of being out of sync. Some people, however, erroneously believe that if they can only get in balance they can live in that comfort zone forever—of course, you can't. As in nature, there is always the striving for balance, but balance itself comes less often than we would like. The fact is, one moves in and out of balance. When you are out of balance, during times of agitation, you are the most likely to be productive and creative. When you are in balance, you will generally feel satisfied and comfortable with yourself, more at peace. You are most apt to forge ahead when you feel uncomfortable and dissatisfied, when you are on the edge of chaos.

EIGHT WAYS TO DEAL WITH YOUR FEARS

No one is without fears. There is fear of failure and fear of success. Fears are natural and often protect us from something bad for us, but they can also block our path to the good things. As you go through life, you constantly exchange old fears for new ones. First we fear that we won't ever get married, then we fear being married; we fear we won't find a good job or that we will find the wrong job. The key is to recognize your fears and befriend them—they tell you a lot about you. Use them as a positive force in your life. Here are some suggestions for handling fear:

1. When you get that anxious feeling in the pit of your stomach, try to focus on what's causing it. Focusing doesn't always work, but it is worth a try. If you are able to isolate the cause of the current feeling of fright, you can do something about it. If I awake during the night with free-floating fear or anxiety and can't identify the cause, I don't lay in bed and suffer. I get up, go to my desk, and try to figure out why it's happening. Sometimes it centers on teaching a class the next day. If that surfaces, I review all my material and make sure I'm prepared. Usually that satisfies the anxiety and I'm able to go back to sleep.

2. Another cause of fear is an unresolved issue. Sometimes the fear persists, but usually, unearthing the cause makes fear manageable. You may be fearful of being fired. This is a hard one to manage because the action is not in your hands—or is it? If you are fearful of getting fired, take some actions to prevent or change the situation. Any actions that will put you in control of the situation will help. When you develop options and alternatives you won't feel at

the mercy of your boss. It may mean preparing your résumé, re-analyzing your
goals, networking for a new position, or
talking to your boss. Once you know
you're not solely at the mercy of the situation your fear will subside.

3. While going through a fearful period it is
    difficult to remember that an ending is also
    a beginning. Out of most every negative
    situation, short of serious illness and death,
    there is a new beginning. Focus on the new
    beginnings and not on the endings to assuage
    or contain your fears.

4. Whenever I am on the horns of a dilemma, I
    experience fear until the dilemma is resolved.
    It is important to recognize the dilemma and
    then try to resolve it. If resolution is not pos-
    sible at the time, think of the fear as energy
    propelling you toward a solution. Imagine it
    flowing toward a positive end.

5. Try a relaxing technique that involves deep
    and controlled breathing that eases the ten-
    sion resulting from your fear. Do this when
    you are about to make a presentation and are
    nervous about it. After all these years, I still
    feel nervous when I am about to give a
    workshop, seminar, or speech. But I have
    learned to turn the fear of not doing well or

of being poorly received into positive energy that I can then put into the presentation. It animates and propels me to give a more dynamic presentation.

6. I learned long ago that physical activity is one of the best ways to dispel fear. When I was younger, I worked out at the gym and played paddleball. When fear hit me, I would work out vigorously and play a hard game of paddleball. Today I do floor exercises, speed walk, and work out with weights. Whatever the physical activity, direct the energy of that fear into activities to dissipate it.

7. Fear feeds the fight or flight reaction that is basic to everyone. There is no better way to escape the clutches of fear than to fight the situation causing it or to remove yourself from it. In Monty Python's *The Quest for the Holy Grail*, when the characters can't handle a situation, they don't say, "retreat," they say, "run away, run away." You must decide, in every fearful situation, whether to stay and fight or run away.

8. Most of the suggestions in the preceding points involve staying and fighting the situation. Try to take charge so that you are in control. Analyze, prepare, plan; take some action to handle the situation. Stepping

away or running away from a situation after you have concluded it is a no-win for you, however, it is as valid a reaction as fighting and sometimes the best thing to do.

There are some fears that require professional help to control. If your fear is deep and uncontrollable, you are wise to seek that help.

AW! YOU HURT MY FEELINGS

"What do you think I am, a sissy?" "What do you mean, I can't control it! I can handle anything you throw my way!" "You can't hurt me; I am Super Person." When you're young, you often feel this way. I did, and I was wrong. My feelings could be hurt, I did bend, and I was fearful—I just could never admit it. My mother misled me. She always said, "There is no such word as can't." Of course, there are many can'ts for each of us in life. Unless you can be truthful and realistic with yourself, and admit the fears, hurts, and can'ts that come your way, it will be difficult to become a success within yourself. You will almost never find an inner comfort zone because you will be shouldering the burden of indestructibility. We are all destructible.

When my first book was published, I proudly gave my Dad a copy. He devastated me by saying, "I could have done that." Naturally I was looking for a pat on the back from the person I most wanted recognition from, or at least to hear, "It's good work, son." I was stunned. Frankly, I didn't know how to handle my feelings. But examining my relationship with my Dad and understanding the kind of man he was, I realized he was not being nasty or malevolent. I realized, too, that he must have been hurt by my accomplishment and, at the same time, proud. In reality, he could have done what I did, but he had not. Because I did it, he must have seen it as a failure or lack of success on his part. My Dad was a loving man and we were very close. I knew it had to be that my achievement had stirred something deep within him and that he was really not attacking me but rather castigating himself. Nevertheless, it took me a long time to get over his remark, for he was the one person from whom I wanted approval.

My hurt feelings and need for my Dad's approval quickly catapulted me into writing another book, one he could not have done. Hurt feelings can get in the way of your success just as they can drive you to success. Each of us is unique and reacts differently to our life experiences. When our feelings have been hurt, we can either react aggressively, fight, shrink from it, or run away. However, if you have a clear picture of your path to the success you have chosen, stick to it, no matter how your feelings are hurt. Use your feelings as a positive propellant toward your goals.

Anyone Can Be a Success

Look over the list of characteristics that lead to success.

- A clear definition of what success is for you.

- An understanding of what it will take to be successful in each of the areas where you want to succeed and an understanding of the talents and abilities you will need.

- Matching your talents and abilities to those that are required.

- Clear goals.

- Believing in yourself.

- Constancy of purpose.

- A strong drive to get there—wherever "there" is for you.

- A willingness to work hard to achieve the success you seek.

- Honesty with yourself and others.

- Courage to face the challenges.

- Feeling that you will be a success always helps, as do positive attitudes in all things.

- Being able to take advantage of serendipity and luck.

> *"...the confidence in success, which not seldom brings actual success with it."*

—Sigmund Freud, *A Childhood Memory of Goethe's* (1916)

The secret of being a success is not the accumulation of money or possessions but the accumulation of feelings of success.

I truly believe anyone can be a success if they have chosen goals that are within their capabilities and talents and are willing to apply themselves, not just wish for success. As Freud wrote, you must have that feeling that you will be a success before you can become a success.

ARE YOU A HOME RUN HITTER OR AN RBI CHAMP?

You don't have to be a home run hitter to be a success. You can, like me, rely on batting in the runs. When I discovered that I did not have the talent nor the temperament for the big deal, I realized that I would have to build my success one run at a time.

Many years ago I asked a well-known and brilliant business journalist I knew, Earl Lifshey, for his criticism of my business activities. He told me that he thought I was "a mile wide and an inch deep." At first I was hurt by his assessment, but as he went on to explain what he meant, I realized he was right. I was building my success over a wide area of activities, filling life's glass a drop at a time. In his view, if I did not concentrate my activities, I would never achieve any great success. I guess he was right. I never did achieve any "great" success, but I did achieve many small ones that added up to what was, for me, a satisfying and successful life.

Why do I say that? Well, first and foremost, I have a loving and wonderful marriage to Gloria, my soulmate, friend, and lover. I take great pride in the kind of man our son Mark is, in the deep reciprocated love we have, and in the love for his wife Isabelle. There is a closeness and love for my younger brother, David, who, because of our age difference, is almost like another son. He was my business partner for most of my life and made me very proud when he took over the sales rep business with his partner. They built it to heights I never could have reached.

I have achieved reasonable success in business. I've made a decent living, accumulated a respectable net worth, provided a platform for others to build upon, became well-known and respected in my areas of work, and, most important, have found my work most satisfying. I have had published over 130 articles and eleven books and have given workshops, seminars, and speeches internationally. I have been consultant to some of the finest Fortune 500 companies. I derive great pleasure from those I have mentored and from my students. My charitable work continues to be rewarding, as well. I have been privileged to travel the world and have dear friends in a number of foreign countries. Yes, I feel very successful. Maybe I'm not a gigantic success to the outside world, but I have success enough to the world I travel in and, more important, success enough to satisfy me.

When I spoke with Earl Lifshey, I was a partner and the president of an independent sales rep agency (the one now run by my brother and his partner); had started a consulting company, which I still operate as a solo practitioner; had a fledgling company in Hong Kong trying to do business with China (it was closed when our partner in Hong Kong died); had a small sales agency in Israel that a partner in Israel and I still operate; had been president of a small automotive accessory manufacturing company (long ago sold off); was operating some real estate we owned; and was writing and lecturing. I was trying to find a multitude of means to accumulate some money, gain recognition within the industry, express my creativity, and cater to my wide range of interests. Perhaps it was a rationalization for trying for the big hit and not hitting it. To this day I'm not sure that if I had followed Earl's advice it would have led to greater financial success and a greater feeling that I was a success. If I had concentrated on only one thing, however, I know I would have become bored and unhappy. In my mind, contrary to what Earl felt,

I was becoming successful because I was achieving my goals, one drop at a time. It worked for me. It might not work for you.

Your need may be to become a home run hitter or to live on the edge to achieve the kind of success you want. I suspect, however, that a drop at a time might be more comfortable for most people. With a drop-at-a-time approach, the small successes from each area in your life add up to feeling that your life is indeed a success. Smacking the occasional home run, however, does give great exhilaration and satisfaction. If that's your thing, go for it.

A glass can be filled slowly or quickly. When you're young, you want to fill it as quickly as possible. As you age, you take pleasure in every drop that fills the glass.

.

4

CHOOSE THE LIFE
YOU LIVE CAREFULLY

Live an active inner life; keep on trying things.

Although serendipity and luck often direct our lives, it does not have to be that way. You have more control of your life than you think—providing you take charge. You may have a job you don't like; you may be unhappy with your home life; or, on the other hand, you may be satisfied with all aspects of your life. The point is, *you can choose the life you live,* if you know what kind of life you want and are willing to work at it. No, it is not always completely attainable. Adjustments to reality must be made. But floating through life is like being on a sailing ship with no one steering. The waves, winds, and storms of life will toss you about and take you who knows where.

If the ship has your firm hand on the tiller, however, you can weather most storms and steer to the port of your choice.

An old story tells of a pious, noble man who asked God to help him win the lottery. He wanted to use the money to aid the poor and destitute. He would talk to God and each time God promised that he would help. But the old man did not win the lottery and complained to the good Lord that the promise had not been kept. A booming voice answered back, "The least you can do is buy a ticket." If you hope to win at anything in life—family, money, career, whatever—the least you can do is buy a ticket. Nothing will happen if you just dream or pray. Life must be engaged. In order to win, you have to participate. Life must be fully lived if you want to choose the direction you want to go.

YOU CAN'T BE SUCCESSFUL IN A DIRTY DIAPER

I wonder how many of you think about how your lives are affected by the environment you choose to live in—the people you associate with, where you live and work, where you worship, and where and how you spend your time. In the time life allows you, where and how you spend your time determines your functioning environment. If it is a negative environment for the success you seek, your life will be like living in a "dirty diaper."

Here are some of the arenas where you will have to choose your operating environment:

- Where you live and your community
- Where you work
- Your schools
- Your friends
- Your associates at work
- The person you choose to love
- The person you marry
- The family you raise
- The religious organization you choose or don't choose to join
- Any and all other areas of life you may be involved with

YOU GOTTA BE YOU

While dining with friends recently I asked the three other people whether they had chosen the life they lived or whether their life had chosen them. Two of us felt we had chosen and the other two did not.

When Russ, a successful accountant, was young, no particular path appealed to him. He studied accounting after a stint in the army because some family members thought it would be a good career. He knew he wanted to get married, have a family, and make enough money to be comfortable, but he was not clear on the kind of work he wanted to do. He said he could just as well have been an attorney. Retired now, he is financially comfortable. He is also enjoying the dividends of a loving family and a young grand-child and feels his life has been successful.

His wife, Susan, felt that she had chosen her life. From the time she was fifteen she remembers that she wanted to be a therapist. Her parents discouraged her from going into psychology, so she became a schoolteacher. She married and, with Russ, built a mutually loving life. When she was in her forties, she went back to school with Russ's support and earned a Masters degree. Today she is a successful therapist who enjoys her work and her family.

Some of us will and do choose and direct the lives we live. Others let life carry them along. Unfortunately, there are many of us who do not know what we want out of life. What can you do if you do not know what you want to do with your life or can't seem to bring about change in the direction you would like to go? Read on.

WHAT IS GOOD FOR ME MAY NOT BE GOOD FOR YOU

As each of us is different, you can run into problems and create tensions for yourself when you try to be what you are not. It's important not to go against your basic nature. For example, I could have been more successful in the early days of establishing our sales rep business if I had participated in offering things that some of our major buyers wanted: gifts, money, women, socializing. I just could not do it—it was against my nature. My interests and what interested most of the people in the industry were not the same. They were good, hard-working people, but I was not in sync with their lifestyles and interests, something I had not factored in when I went into business. In fact, I had not considered the work environment or the people I would have to work with. The diversion of interests proved to be a negative in establishing our business, and more important, in the satisfaction I could obtain from my day-to-day activities.

The people I dealt with were, for the most part, decent people, but they did not provide me with the stimulation and challenges I needed. After the sales rep agency was established, this lack was the primary reason that I gravitated to consulting, where the work was more challenging and the people I came into contact with were more interesting. Happily, it turned out that the two businesses were synergistic. That fact, as well as economic reasons, kept us running both businesses for many years. While the rep agency produced more business, consulting produced more personal satisfaction. I was using our business activities primarily to satisfy my needs and, secondly, to make money.

Our sales rep business was established in 1956 and our consulting company in 1968. Then, in 1975, my life changed dramatically. I was diagnosed with severe arthritis of my spine and had the first of four major operations. I was fortunate to have my brother as a partner and that we had built a good team of people. My brother began to take charge of the rep business and I began to devote more time to consulting, which was physically less strenuous than selling. In 1987 I sold my interest in the sales agency and took over my brother's interest in the consulting company. He went on to build a highly successful business with a young partner. I adapted the consulting to my physical limitations. To this day I continue to write, arbitrate, and teach at New York University as an adjunct associate professor, one class a semester—I'm finally doing everything I wanted to do. My brother is also doing what he wanted to do and what he excels at.

CRITICAL PERIODS IN LIFE

Looking back over the years, I realize that the following periods in our lives are critical. The decisions you make during these periods can be turning points:

High School: What you decide to do in high school is the first critical choice you make. Prior to that time, most choices are directed by your parents or other adults. During those high school years, you can choose to just take up space or you can work on a foundation for your education and your life. It is during this time that the influence of peers, family, and friends can put you on the right track or point you in the wrong direction. It is not likely that you will have figured out what is best without some help from older and wiser people. Even then, it can be difficult to know what you want to do with your life. Will you get a job, learn a craft, or prepare for college? Will you learn how to study and interact with people, or will you rebel and just try to get by? It is not likely that a conscious decision was made by the child/adult you were. I hope you had good instincts and guidance from trusted adults in your life.

Graduation: When you finish high school, you must make conscious decisions that affect your life. You will decide, probably with strong input from your parents, whether to work or go to college. If you are one of the lucky ones, you will know what you want to do. If you are not, like many young people, going to college can open up new areas of interest that may lead to a decision. Learning how to think and to prepare yourself with a good education will help you succeed in whatever you ultimately choose.

College: The college you choose, the courses you take, the lifetime friends you make, the contacts you develop, will all provide you with tools for your future life.

Leaving Home: When you leave your parent's home to live on your own, the people you associate with and what you work toward are critical to where you will arrive later in life.

People You Associate With: The women or men you date, the friends you make, and the people you choose to spend time with create the environment in which you will be making your decisions.

Your First Job: Your first full-time employment can affect how you feel and how you react to this initial opportunity. Will it be a position where you will learn or will it be one where learning is secondary to producing?

Career Development: With a little luck, you will be working on your career. It may be just what you expected or you may be disappointed in your choice. Don't worry if it proves disappointing. Worrying is a waste of time and energy. Rethink your goals and make a planned change to a new area of work. I had to change and add to my business activities. At some point in life, you may want a second career.

Marriage and Family: Your values and the values you develop as a family are major influences in setting life directions. Who you choose as your closest friend, life partner, lover, and companion should be based on more than just passion. There should be a fit of interests, principles, morals, ethics, respect, love, and values.

Other Critical Times: You can be certain that there will be other critical times for decisions in your life. Your first child, an illness, a death in the family, economic setbacks, and more can become critical decision-making times. During these critical times, it is most important to remember that the impact of the event will pass. Life can and will go on. In the adversity of critical times, there is always the possibility of a new beginning.

CREATIVE TENSION

If everything goes your way, it is not likely that you will change and grow to the same degree as when tensions develop. Usually it is when things are out of balance and not perfect that you are the most creative and undertake new actions. A fascinating book is *At Home in The Universe: The Search for the Laws of Self-Organization and Complexity* by Stuart Kaufman (Oxford University Press, 1995). He theorizes that order in the universe evolves at the edge of chaos. We can apply this concept to our lives. On the edge of chaos is where new order develops for us, too. When we are in the throes of complete chaos, we tend to freeze up. But when we are at its edge, we are stimulated. I call this period *creative tension,* which moves us into new areas of thought, creativity, and action. In my consulting practice I often try to induce creative tension into situations in order to break paradigms. If you use it creatively, your tension will help you redirect your life toward your goals.

When tensions strike, try the following techniques to turn them into creative tensions:

- Regroup your inner strengths.
- Remember that this is not an end, but a beginning.
- Thoroughly analyze the situation.
- Avoid the negatives; turn toward the positive aspects of the tension.
- Believe even harder in yourself.
- Hold on to your goals.
- Hold in check your fear of going into uncharted areas.
- Think positively.
- Move to action; don't procrastinate.

These suggestions are easy to list but difficult to do. If, however, you keep your wits about you and look at tensions as creative opportunities, you will have a choice of actions.

MONKEY SEE! MONKEY DO!

It is natural to copy successful people. There is no cookbook for success, however. You can gather ideas and review what others have done, but you will not find that someone else's approach will work for you. Books like this one that try to help bring success into your life can only act as guides. You must adjust and adapt my suggestions and only adopt the ones that fit your unique needs.

Intangibles like integrity, honesty, industriousness, fortitude, and persistence are worth adopting. It is difficult to practice these characteristics, however, if they are not part of your nature. But with effort and awareness on your part, you can do it. Religion, the preserver of socially recognized values, helps some people. How you apply these characteristics, when you apply them and to what degree, is your decision. Misapplication has its consequences and, at this stage in your life, you are the sole keeper of right or wrong.

WHAT PARTS OF YOUR LIFE CAN YOU CHOOSE AND WHAT PARTS CHOOSE YOU?

*God, give us the grace to accept with serenity
the things that cannot be changed, courage to
change the things which should be changed,
and the wisdom to distinguish the one from
the other.*

—Reinhold Niebuhr, *The Serenity Prayer* (1943)

You can change those parts of your life that allow you to choose. The things you can't change and must learn to accept are usually the things that have chosen you. You can't always be in control when you are affected by illness, someone's death, or the behavior of others. But you can change how you allow these things to affect you and your reaction to them. Confused? I think you will understand what I mean when I relate what happened to me.

In January 1975, when I began to lose neurological functions, I had a laminectomy that I hoped would cure my chronic and debilitating lower spine back pain. In November of that same year, I had another laminectomy. In March 1976, I had a fusion of disks in my neck; in February 1997, I had fusions in my lower spine and an opening of my spinal column to allow more room for the spinal cord nerves.

Osteoarthritis was devastating me. I spent almost a year in bed after the last surgery and another year riding around in an electric cart. I was, and still am, always in pain. In May 1980, I fractured my hip. In April 1991, cancer was detected in my prostate, and a month later, I had a radical prostratectomy. I have been cancer free since. All in all, including other stints of surgery, I have undergone 11 operations. There are people who have had more and many who have had less—but that is not the point. The point is, what did I learn from these things that had chosen me?

I learned that I had no choice; the disease got me. I learned that wallowing in self-pity and lying around made me feel worse than when I was engaged in life. My reaction was my choice. I chose to continue working through all of the attacks. I worked from my hospital bed at home and from a couch in my office. On one occasion, just home from the hospital, I spent a day consulting at my bedside for Stanadyne/Moen Faucets. Other consultations took place by phone. I was in constant contact with my office. Because I kept taking care of my business responsibilities, I felt wanted and needed.

The strangest consulting assignment I ever had was with our client Honeywell. Although they knew of my condition, they insisted that I fly to Minneapolis for a consultation. They said it was an emergency. I made the trip, walking up and down the aisle on the plane most of the time as sitting was too difficult.

When I arrived, I went straight to the hotel and rested that day and night. The next day they picked me up. I did my consulting lying on a conference table, with everyone sitting around the table. It was the weirdest meeting I have ever experienced. At the end of the day, I rested and flew home the next day. Although I was in a great deal of pain, I felt I was valuable and beginning to take charge of my disorder and limitations.

For many years I was on all sorts of medication to help me get through the day. I worked as much as I could and kept as active as possible: I was not going to give in. Finally, after about ten years of heavy medication, I decided, with the help and urging of my doctor, to kick the pills. I started physical and psychological therapy, tried biofeedback, relaxation techniques, acupuncture, and more. With perseverance I kicked the medication and only used it when major attacks occurred. Regular exercise and a positive frame of mind brought my pain level from a 6 or 7 on a scale of 1 to 10 down to where it is now, a very livable 3 or 4.

I chose to fight and not give in. It was during those years of fighting that I was most prolific, traveled the most, and earned more money than before the onset of the disease. That's what I mean by choosing. You can always choose how to react, even when you can't choose what happens to you.

DEALING WITH THE ANGER WITHIN

Anger is a powerful force. It can destroy or give energy, which can then be harnessed and directed. You can well imagine the anger I felt each time I had to undergo surgery. If I turned the anger inward, it would eat me up. If I turned it outward, it would eat up my family and friends. It was difficult; for a while I couldn't find a place for my anger. I noticed, however, that when I was fully engaged—working, writing, teaching, or whatever—the anger transformed into energy, which I was then able to use constructively. It probably would have been easier to go around angry with myself and the world, but I knew that wouldn't bring me to the life I wanted to lead.

It takes great awareness of your inner self to know, first, why you are angry and, second, how to direct that anger constructively. It took time for me to realize and to acknowledge that when a minor incident triggered a tirade directed at my wife, son, or anyone else, they were not the source of my anger. After a while, when I lost control, I was able to acknowledge that I was not angry with them, I was angry at being in so much pain. I asked forgiveness for taking it out on them.

Once, on a plane trip, someone moved my bag from under the seat in front of me. I couldn't bend because of my back, but I kept trying to reach it. I was fuming. An older man leaned over, picked up my bag, and handed it to me. This made me even angrier. He said, "You know, it isn't so terrible to accept help. When you do, you make me feel good that I can help you and, you know, we all need help one time or another." He was right! From that day on I never got angry when I had to ask for help or was helped. I also found I enjoyed helping others more than I had before this brief encounter.

When anger wells up in your belly, it is difficult to think rationally. Only after the anger has subsided can you begin to talk with yourself and ask the following questions:

- Why did I get angry?

- Was it really this incident that triggered my anger, or was it just a trigger for the anger that was already brewing inside me?

- Who did I direct the anger at?

- Why did I direct the anger at that person?

- Was the anger appropriately directed?

- How did I feel after the anger subsided?

- What could I have done with the anger that might have turned out to be constructive?

OH, THAT EGO!

The ego is the self as contrasted to others. It is where your self-esteem resides. The Id is the unconscious driving force of your instinctual needs.

The ego's relation to the Id might be compared with that of a rider [the ego] to his horse [the Id]. The horse supplies the locomotive energy, while the rider has the privilege of deciding on the goal and of guiding the powerful animal's movement.

—Sigmund Freud, *New Introductory Lectures on Psycho-analysis,*
1933, Lecture 31

Our ego gives us strength but also can get in the way of complete honesty with ourselves. With a healthy ego, it is easier to choose the life you live and to be successful. That's why it's important to strengthen your ego by undertaking tasks that, when successfully completed, will give you a positive image of yourself.

We all have a varying amount of ego strength and ego drive. Ego strength is having sufficient self-worth to pick yourself up when you have been rejected or failed. It is the strength of the ego that enables us to face adversity because it tells us we are worthy, we are strong, we can do it—try again. Ego drive is what pushes us to acquire more self-esteem. Without it, we would not reach higher. Our ego drive is what calls us to be successful, to gain recognition, and to want to achieve.

In an article in the *New York Times Health Section* on May 5, 1998, Kirk Johnson, the author of *Self-Image Is Suffering From Lack Of Esteem,* says:

Common sense and research had shown that people who did best in life felt good about themselves, and it seemed a short leap to conclude that the reverse must also be true: If successful people enjoyed high self-esteem, then high self-esteem would foster success.

A word of caution: High self-esteem should come from achievements if it is going to lead to success. Just thinking positively about oneself will not do it. Trying to develop self-esteem in people will not do it. There has to be a constant doing and achieving. This is why some people with low self-esteem can be successful, for their ego drives them to find successes.

Here is a test of self-esteem that I have devised, based on the work done by Morris Rosenberg in his book *Conceiving the Self* (Basic Books, 1979).

		YES	NO
1.	I am satisfied with who and what I am.	_____	_____
2.	I have a positive attitude toward myself.	_____	_____
3.	I am as worthy as others.	_____	_____
4.	In general, I do things as well as most people.	_____	_____
5.	I have something to be proud of.	_____	_____

If you checked all five as YES, you have healthy self-esteem. If YES is checked only three times, it indicates that you're probably OK with yourself, but could use some work in building more self-esteem. Fewer than three indicates you need a lot of work on your self-esteem.

The best way I know of to work on self-esteem is to screw up your courage and take on tasks that will make you proud of yourself. It is only by doing and achieving that a sound level of self-esteem can be reached. To choose your life and not let it choose you means to not be passive and to accept what life sends your way. It means choosing things that you may never have done before, things you are afraid of, things that take you into new areas, things that will help you attain your goals.

Part II

Wishing Alone Won't Do It—Planning Will

Plan for your success.

5

WISHING ALONE WON'T DO IT

The most successful people in life are the ones who know what they want out of life... who they want to be. They have a clear vision of their hopes and dreams.

W hen I taught Strategic Planning at New York University's Marketing and Management Institute, every semester I introduced my students to my personal planning system. To this day, whenever I hold workshops on strategic planning, I introduce the subject from a personal planning perspective. I strongly believe that planning—*making written plans*—makes wishes come to life. Therefore, I developed the LifePlan system.

A Planning System that Works—If You Use It

During a workshop on LifePlan, a husband and wife team who own a small chain of furniture stores told the group that they were having trouble planning for the future of their business. After the lunch break, the wife said, *"A simple but potent revelation came to my husband and me during the morning session of the workshop. We realized that we first have to decide what we want from life before we can decide what we want from our business."*

Entrepreneurs of small and medium-sized companies often cannot state a clear vision for their companies, let alone their company goals and strategies. Since most entrepreneurs operate their businesses to satisfy their life's needs and dreams, they must first know what their life goals are. Only then can they derive personal satisfaction from their businesses and lead their companies to success. This is true whatever you do with your life.

LifePlan is a way to self-fulfillment. If you are not clear what to do next with your life—what direction you want your life to take; where to lead your career, profession, or business; how to realize your fantasies— or even when you do know what you want but never seem able to achieve it, the LifePlan system can help. Though the process is simple, it may not always be easy to get yourself to do it. Like everything of value, it takes discipline. But once you've gone through the process, it's easy to maintain a LifePlan.

This section of the book is devoted to the LifePlan system, a methodology for personal planning that consists of the following tasks:

- Establishing a personal vision.

- Developing a personal mission.

- Analyzing your situation through an analysis of your likes, dislikes, strengths, and weaknesses.

- Setting your personal goals.

- Assigning strategies to your personal goals.

- Monitoring and measuring your success.

- Setting a timetable for it all to happen.

A FIST IS BETTER THAN A FINGER

Think of the fingers of your hand as your resources; for example, your education, training, abilities, family. If you don't plan, it is like extending one finger (one resource) at a time to strike a particular target or goal. If you plan, it is like pulling the five fingers of your hand (all of your resources) into a fist and directing it toward what you want to achieve— your goals or aims. It will have impact in whatever direction you aim your fist.

Dwight D. Eisenhower said, *"Plans are nothing, planning is everything."* Plans themselves are often useless, but *the planning process is always vital.* The process forces you to analyze and to think through the things that lead to a plan. It requires step-by-step analysis. It forces you to face yourself, to look at your likes and dislikes, your strengths and weaknesses, your hopes and dreams, and goals you may not realize you have. Most of the time you will come up with a workable plan. Sometimes you will find that the plan you develop is just not workable. If that happens, go back over the process, reexamine each step, study your worksheets to see where you may have gone off track, and then see how you can develop a more workable new plan.

PLANNING: CONTENT AND PROCESS

Planning is assembling all your resources, setting goals, and developing clear actions or strategies to achieve them.

CONTENT

Content is the hard detail of the plan—the goals, strategies, and evaluations that you set down on paper. This chapter, as well as chapters 6 and 7, is devoted to helping you develop the content of your plan. The LifePlan system is primarily a process to help you determine the content of the plan.

PROCESS

Process is the part of planning where you think, conceptualize, and make decisions that lead to your goals and strategies. It also includes interaction with others to discuss your ideas and share your thoughts and feelings. Your mind is at work taking in and analyzing information that you can put down on paper. The process of planning happens conceptually, not linearly. You should move back and forth freely through the process until your conclusions are satisfactory. The process is also circular, moving from ideas to goals, often giving rise to other ideas that, in turn, give rise to new or different goals. As I wrote in my book, *10 Minute Guide to Planning* (Alpha Books, 1997), the process of planning is important because it makes you think. Of course, you need to have a plan in hand when you have gone through the process, and you will. Keep in mind, however, that the process is never ending. You must monitor and change the plan as circumstances dictate and as elements of the plan work or fail. It is, however, this process of analyzing, planning, monitoring, and re-planning that is all-important.

The Never Ending Planning Cycle will initially follow in the direction of the arrows. As you work your plan, from time to time you may need to break into the circle and reevaluate one or more of the planning elements. For example, after you establish your goals, you may want to go back and change

The Never Ending Planning Cycle

your mission to more accurately reflect your goals, or vice versa. For this plan to be fully useful, think of it as a living document, something that reminds, guides, and gives direction. As circumstances change, plans must also change.

EIGHT QUESTIONS TO ASK WHEN PLANNING

There are eight questions basic to planning that you must answer in greater detail to get the most out of the planning process.

1. WHERE AM I NOW?

Where you want to be may already be reflected in "Where am I now?" In other words, you may be where you want to be now. For example, if you want to be a physician and are in your third year of medical school, you are on the way to where you want to be—a physician. However, you may not yet have chosen a special area in which to practice medicine. You are at the crossroads of choosing your specialty. What you choose will be where you want to be and how you will spend your life's work as a doctor. The decision you make about your specialty is where you ultimately want to be.

I remember when all I could think of was getting a job, any job, in order to feed my family. Although I had started a business, it was not earning enough to put bread on the table. My primary goal became bringing in additional money. I landed a part-time job in a shoe store and worked nights and weekends. Even if this cut into getting my business established—where I really wanted to be—I had to accept the fact that finding a way to earn enough to keep us going until the business was established was where I was. I knew where I was and I knew where I wanted to be. Whatever I planned to do to get that business established had to be built from where I was.

Elements in planning overlap; planning tends to be circular in nature. If, however, you don't know where you are, it is like planning a journey to New

York without knowing your starting point. There is no way to navigate from that position. You don't know the direction to go in, the form of transportation to take, or how long it will take you to get there. The starting point for any plan is always, "where are you now?"

2. WHERE DO I WANT TO BE?

You may have a vague idea of where you want to be, but you need a specific list to bring your goals into focus. Call it a wish list, if you like. I call it goals or end aims. Make your list realistic. Your wishes must be based on research, the most logical assumptions you can make, and careful analysis. If you don't know where you want to be, you will find the SWLD (strengths, weaknesses, likes, and dislikes) exercise later in this chapter helpful in ferreting out where you want to be as life moves on.

Most people are misemployed, not unemployed. To avoid being one of the misemployed, pay attention to the characteristics of the work you like to do, not to the image of the job. It may seem glamorous to be a model, athlete, performer, or to work in broadcasting, advertising, publishing, or some other high-profile profession. When you look into what is involved in becoming a person with a "glamorous" position, however, you might find that what you need to get there is not for you. If, for example, you know that you want to become an attorney, find out what an attorney's life is really like. Don't judge the requirements for the profession or its daily activities by what you see on television, in the movies, or read about in the press. Learn how real attorneys function and what kind of work they do. Determine what you do and don't like about law. Writing briefs may be good for one person; for someone else, trial work is best. Only by visiting courts and attorneys' offices and by checking with law schools can you begin to get a realistic picture of what the daily life of a lawyer is really like.

You must always research what you think you want in order to be sure that what you imagine it to be is in fact what it is.

3. How Will I Get There?

What strategies will you need to develop to reach your established goals? Strategies are the means you use to obtain your goals. It is "how you get there." How you get there is as important as where you are going, if not more so. If the means are not realistic, if the hardship is too great, if the discipline required is beyond what is worthwhile, if you don't have the resources, or if for any other reason it is too difficult to implement, rethink your strategies. If there are no apparent alternative strategies, you may have to change your goal or goals.

Few of us have sufficient resources to be able to do everything we want to do, especially all at the same time. That's why it's important to prioritize your strategies and your goals. Chapters 6 and 12 include forms for developing goals and strategies that include ranking.

4. WHEN DO I WANT TO ARRIVE?

What are your priorities? What are your most important goals? Are you willing to sacrifice one particular goal for another? Which goal do you want to achieve first, second, third? When do you want to achieve each of your goals? When do you expect to accomplish each of your goals? Prepare a schedule or calendar noting when you expect certain acts to occur. Be sure to check how they tie in with your other activities. Chapter 7 discusses this more fully.

If you are the kind of person who feels more comfortable with a set schedule or timetable for your actions, develop a flow chart that lists the things you want to do and when you want them done. LifePlan can be as simple as a list of goals and strategies or it can encompass the entire planning process. If you like to work things out in detail, develop a flow chart. If not, just list a time frame next to each goal. Either way, the important thing is to have some idea of when you will reach your goals.

5. WHO WILL HELP GET ME THERE?

You are the one responsible for your LifePlan; you are the one who has to make it happen. Once you know what you want and how you are going to get it, you will probably need help getting there. If you

lack resources, try networking. Take advantage of
your contacts and your contacts' contacts to give you
a long, strong reach. Reach out to friends, business
and professional contacts, and others for valuable
input and to test your ideas. Networking provides
additional resources to help bring your LifePlan into
successful action.

Networking is an important part of planning.
Though we all like to think we get where we do in
life through our own abilities, often we get a leg up
from our contacts. Sometimes a phone call to someone
you know gives you the critical information or advice
you need. Other times a contact gets you an appoint-
ment with a person you want to meet. A good book
on networking is *Network Your Way To Success* by
Ken Erdman and Tom Sullivan (Marketers Bookshelf, 402 Bethlehem Pike, Philadelphia, PA 19118;
phone: 215-247-2787; fax: 215-233-2203.)

For many years I have kept a database of my contacts. I used to do this mechanically, using business
cards and notes. Since computers are everywhere, I
have built a database for mailings. E-mail, phone
contacts, and general correspondence allow me to
easily access groups of people who may impact what
I need at any particular time. I keep a log of key contacts in my database. I also have a reminder system
that alerts me when to send a birthday card, make a
phone contact, drop an e-mail, or make some other
contact. If you do not have some sort of database to

record, sort, and log information about contacts, start
one now.

6. WHAT WILL IT COST?

The commitment you make to your LifePlan will
cost you—in time, possibly in money, but mostly in
emotional investment. No plan can be brought to
reality without some cost. You are making a deep
emotional investment. Don't set yourself up for
failure. Be realistic so that what you invest in your
LifePlan can bear fruit. You will be investing time,
your family's time and emotions, and resources. It is
not possible to develop a LifePlan and not have it
affect those close to you. There is usually a dollar and
cents investment as well. What is the risk and what is
the return benefit of each of your actions?

In the form for developing goals and strategies in
Chapter 6, you will see the questions "What will it
cost?" and "What is the expected return?" These important questions help you to focus on the cost
return aspect of your plan.

7. HAVE I GOT WHAT IT TAKES AND WILL I LIKE IT?

Too often we have vague road maps in mind to lead
us to our important aims in life. Without clear and
precise road maps, you are unlikely to achieve your
goals. With no understanding of your own strengths
and weaknesses and your likes and dislikes, you have
no way of knowing whether you can travel the road

you have mapped out for yourself and, more importantly, whether you will enjoy the trip. Only when you have analyzed your strengths and weaknesses, likes and dislikes, can you determine whether your goals are achievable. Use the worksheets later in this chapter to make an analysis. It is essential to go through this exercise—it is the backbone of personal planning.

8. WHAT WILL SUCCESS BE?

At one time, my consulting company took on a major assignment with Entergy Corporation, the third or fourth largest electric utility company in America, to help them devise a process for developing new products and services. When I met with their CEO, Edward Lupberger, and asked him what he thought success would be for the project, he said it would be when the new product development process was installed and operating. At that time, Entergy had several operating companies, each headed by a president. When interviewing each of the presidents, I asked the same question. As people responsible for the bottom line for their operating company, they all answered with a specific dollar figure that the investment in the process should produce.

The development team that established the installation considered getting the new product process up and running as "success." Now we had to change the meaning of "success" to having the new products or services produce a certain amount of dollar return in addition to being up and running. As our budget for establishing this process came from the operating companies, it was perfectly understandable that they would not be happy without a certain return for the money they invested, while the CEO would be happy to have an operating system. The point is that each of us has a different idea about what success is. Unless you know what it is for you, your plan cannot take into account what you want for success.

Know what success will be for each part of your plan. If you don't, you may not recognize success when it arrives. More important, you won't be able to monitor and measure your progress to help keep on track. It's not necessary to monitor your goals and strategies daily, but look at them periodically to see if you are on target. A complete LifePlan review and any necessary changes should be done annually.

GETTING STARTED

Some of us are fortunate to know clearly what our life goals are and how we will accomplish them. Most of us, however, do not. If you are among the fortunate few, then it is relatively simple to develop a LifePlan. For everyone else, start with a list of your goals. Keep in mind that goals change, so this first list should be flexible. Later, when your goals firm up, they should not easily be changed. For now, this list of goals will serve as your first rough draft.

Remember, your list must be written. Unless you commit your goals to paper, the system will not work. After you have a firm list of goals, take another piece of paper and draw a vertical line down the center of the page. Head one column "Goals" and the other "Strategies." It will look similar to the following figure. Select one goal from your goal list and put it under "Goals." In the next column, write all the strategies you can think of to accomplish that specific goal. Then choose those strategies you will actually use to accomplish the goal. Next, list your second goal and appropriate strategies. Then move on to your third goal. Don't underestimate the importance of developing very personal goals and strategies. They provide a clear vision of how to turn your dreams and fantasies into reality.

Goals are where you want to get and the strategies are how you get there. Sometimes a goal can become a strategy and vice versa. For example, set a goal—start my own business. Your strategy—get a job in the field in which I expect to start the business. Getting the job can become a goal itself with its own set of strategies. When a strategy is to network with people in the industry, it might convert to a goal—get myself known in the industry. For our purpose, it is not technically important that goals and strategies meet clear definitions. What is important is to have clear goals and strategies. The system should not be more important than what you want to achieve.

A note of caution: Don't tackle too many goals at one time. Have a short list. Allow goals to remain fairly fixed. True, goals are not cast in stone and can and should be changed if appropriate. Consider any goal changes carefully.

Sample Listing of Hypothetical Goals and Strategies

AIMS OR GOALS		ACTIONS OR STRATEGIES
1.	**Make a million dollars.**	A. Become a successful entrepreneur.
		B. Get a position in my field and learn all I can on the job.
		C. Finish my formal schooling.
		D. Build up my capital through saving and prudent investment.
		E. Work toward a partnership in the company I am with and/or be prepared to go into my own business.
2.	**Spend more time with my family.**	A. Take a vacation for at least two weeks every year with loved ones.
		B. Go away on a long weekend every three months.
		C. Attend 90 percent of my child's Little League games.

Sample Listing of Hypothetical Goals
   and Strategies (Continued)

AIMS OR GOALS		ACTIONS OR STRATEGIES
3. **Write a book.**	A.	First write articles and get published. (This can also become a goal.)
	B.	Get up one hour earlier every day to write.
	C.	Take a course in writing.
	D.	Talk to writers and find out how they work.

HOW TO DO A SELF-ANALYSIS: DO A SWLD

If you don't know what your goals are, it will help you develop them if you make a list of your *strengths, weaknesses, likes,* and *dislikes (SWLD).* If you do know what your goals and strategies are, go through the SWLD exercise to see if they fit your likes and strengths. Use the worksheet on the next page as a guide for developing and working on your lists.

After you write down a list for strengths, weaknesses, and likes and dislikes, cross-reference your likes with your strengths and your dislikes with your weaknesses. Many people say they have thought through what they want to do and know how they

STRENGTHS	WEAKNESSES
LIKES	DISLIKES

SWLD worksheet/guide

will achieve it. Thinking it through, but not committing it to paper, is only a brush with rational planning. It is food for thought but not an organization of resources, nor an analysis of the situation, nor an examination of your feelings.

The next figure is a hypothetical example of what such a list looks like. I have only listed a few points— your list will be longer. In this example, all the likes can be cross-referenced with the strengths and most of the dislikes with the weaknesses. Where your likes and strengths match, you have a good indication of what you would like to do and would also be good at. From dislikes and weaknesses, you will know what to avoid. This worksheet should trigger some ideas of what you would like to do and would be good at doing. It will often give rise to your goals.

STRENGTHS	WEAKNESSES
1. Analytical	1. Not people-oriented
2. Express myself in writing	2. Not a good public speaker
3. Problem solver	3. Not emotional enough
LIKES	**DISLIKES**
1. Problem solving	1. Irrational thinking
2. Writing	2. Public speaking
3. New technologies	3. A lot of conversation

A Partially Completed Hypothetical Worksheet

TWELVE TRIGGER QUESTIONS TO HELP YOU SEE YOURSELF

To help complete your SWLD, review where you are now in your life. Sounds easy, but it isn't. Try to feel through what your life is like and how you see it. What is its purpose for you? For some of us, the only purpose in life is to make money. For others, the purpose of their lives is to love and be loved; for others, to avoid pain and seek pleasure. Some dedicate their lives to doing what they most enjoy with those who enjoy the same things. Think about what you want out of life—the things that make you happy. Think about the environment you have chosen for yourself—your work environment and your life environment.

1. What is life's purpose?
2. What are the things you like most?
3. What do you dislike?
4. What kind of environment do you want to live in?
5. What are you good at?
6. What are your weaknesses?
7. What vision do you have for yourself?
8. What are the critical issues in your life?

9.   What are your skills and/or talents?

10. What are your competencies?

11. What is most important to you: money, doing what you like, family, where you live, recognition, security, being safe?

12. Where do you want to be one year, three years, and five years from now? Where would you like to be ten years from now?

Think about how others may compete with you for your goals. What are their strengths and weaknesses? How capable are they? Are they a real threat? Can the competition be overcome? How can you prepare yourself so your goals prevail? What are the opportunities you see as a result of this self-analysis? Soon a clear picture of what you really want and are good at will begin to emerge.

LET YOUR BEST FRIEND HELP YOU

Check these lists, particularly your SWLD, with a close friend to see whether you have been honest with yourself. Perhaps he or she can add some points to your lists you are not aware of. I remember one student telling me that when he wrote that he liked classical music, his best friend, his wife, challenged him. She asked why he never played it on the stereo or went to concerts, and when he had last listened to it. It made him realize that liking classical music was an "idealized" preference and that he just thought he should like it. His real music love was jazz. Another person told me that she had not listed performing or speaking in public under her likes. Her best friend asked her why she had left that out. She always said she loved it when she had to speak at meetings or give workshops.

We aren't always honest with ourselves and often need someone we trust and respect to call our attention to what we say and what, in reality, we do.

Zap! It's a Plan!

If you have followed my advice, you have researched, analyzed, made lists, and developed goals and strategies. But is it a plan? Yes, indeed it is if you have set priorities, established timetables, and most important, are implementing this plan. If you write a long involved plan and it sits on your shelf or in a drawer, you may have a plan, but it isn't necessarily a working plan. If you have developed a plan, written it on one or even a few sheets of paper that you keep in your pocket or in a place where you look at it often, then you are more likely to be involved in implementing it. Long-winded plans are not as readily used as simple to-the-point plans. That doesn't mean that little work has gone into the succinct version of a plan. For most people, it is more difficult to write a short letter or book on a complicated topic than to write long ones. You need to know more to develop the plan and to be successful in life. We will talk about this in the next few chapters.

> *We never know how high we are*
> *Till we are called to rise*
> *And then, if we are true to plan*
> *Our statures touch the skies*

—Emily Dickinson, No. 1176 (c. 1870)

6

YOUR LIFE'S MISSION: WILL YOUR GOALS GET YOU THERE?

What is popularity? What is power?
Without a clear mission, there is nothing.

—Warren Beatty, talking about his film "Bulworth,"
New York Times, May 10, 1998

If the gods of popularity and power take hold of you when you have no mission, you will be a slave to repeating the past. By establishing and following your mission, you can change direction, establish values, and define your life's purpose. The mission you set for yourself, if you follow it, directs your life's efforts toward a chosen direction—your vision or your dreams.

Why You Need to Know Your Mission in Life

Have you ever been in this situation? You are changing jobs and are offered two entirely different opportunities. Each will lead in a different direction and each will require different daily tasks. It happened to me.

Early in my marriage a distant cousin who controlled many beer companies, hotels, and other businesses offered me a position with a brewery down South. He added that after he trained me, I would run his brewery. The alternative I was considering was starting my own business. As I had no capital, this alternative was a problem. When my wife and I discussed the two options, we agreed that we didn't like the idea of being beholden to this cousin, who was known for nefarious dealings. I probably would have to do business his way, which was unacceptable to me. Besides, we really didn't want to live in the South, nor did we want to put our fate in someone else's hands, even though a good salary was involved. We knew it would make our lives much easier working for my cousin, but we also knew it did not fit our mission: to establish our own business where we controlled our destiny, values, and actions. We did not take the position with the beer company; instead, we started our own company.

BET YOU THOUGHT MISSIONS WERE ONLY FOR BUSINESSES

Companies often have different names for their mission statement: Corporate Values, Corporate Philosophy, Corporate Statement, Way of Doing Business, among others. The names are interchangeable; the definitions are not important. A horse is a horse, even if you call it something else. Content is what's important. For example, the 3M Company has a Values Statement that outlines their corporate values:

We are committed to: Satisfying our customers with superior quality and value, Providing investors with an attractive return through sustained, high-quality growth, Respecting our social and physical environment, Being a company that employees are proud to be a part of.

The Arthritis Foundation's mission statement:

Support research to find the cure for and prevention of arthritis and to improve the quality of life for those affected by arthritis.

My students often claim that companies have missions, individuals don't. Not true! Individuals should, can, and do have missions in their lives. Sometimes they don't know what their mission is because they have not thought through the key issues. Companies develop mission statements as a means of knowing what they are setting forth to accomplish, just as you should know what you are setting forth to accomplish with your life. Companies share their mission with employees, customers, suppliers, stockholders, and others from whom they want to obtain support and involvement. You, too, need to share your mission with your family and anyone who can affect the accomplishment of your mission.

Here is an example of what might have been my personal mission statement early in my life (if someone had suggested that I develop one):

> ***To be in a deeply dedicated relationship with a loving, caring, and loyal family and friends, based on honesty, integrity, understanding, consideration, and respect; To build a successful business that reflects the same values that I devote to my family and friends; To grow as an individual and be the best that I can at whatever I do.***

Later in life my mission became:

> ***To love and be loved, to pursue intellectual activity, to achieve more than most, to live a life of integrity and honesty, to avoid pain and seek what pleases me, and to give back to the society I live in.***

What is your mission? Can you put it down on paper? Try to develop one now! Then read on and use the six questions in the next section to see if you have thought of everything you might want to incorporate into your mission statement. Review the likes and strengths that you worked on in the last chapter. Are they reflected in your mission? Go over the goals you developed. Do they work with the mission you are developing? Should you change the goals? If so, now is the time to do it, for the goals you establish after you have developed your mission statement should not be changed easily.

SIX QUESTIONS TO ASK YOURSELF ABOUT YOUR MISSION

Your individual mission statement should be a simple written document that sets forth who you are (your values) and what you have set out to do (your goals). Here are six questions to answer:

1. **What are my core values?** Core values are how you feel about honesty, integrity, openness, loyalty, greed, deception, and the cost of achieving them. Remember, your core values define you.

2. **What is my life's business?** It is what you really want to get out of life.

3. **How will I use my resources?** Reality requires an honest appraisal of your skills, talents, money available, capabilities, and other resources.

4. **What is my philosophy of life?** We all have a basic philosophy in approaching life. For some it is greed, achieving at any cost, and what they can get away with. For others it is honesty, integrity, loyalty, and friendship.

5. **In what direction do I want my life to go?** Your vision should provide the clue to the direction in which you want your life to go.

6. **What goals do I want to include in my mission?** If you have worked on some of your goals, as suggested in the last chapter, you know what they are. If you don't, revisit Chapter 5. Also, see the next section in this chapter on goals.

WHAT A MISSION STATEMENT CONTAINS

In my book, *10 Minute Guide to Planning,* there is a guide depicting what a business mission statement should contain. Although I developed this guide for organizations, it translates well for individuals. The comments in **bold italic** apply to individuals.

1. Purpose or reason the organization exists. ***Purpose or reason the individual exists.***

2. Type of products or services offered. ***What the individual has to offer others.***

3. Its markets and customers. *Who you have to convince to accept you and your plans.*

4. How the organization will treat customers. *How you will treat others.*

5. Its values and philosophy. *Your values and philosophy.*

6. The broad direction it will take. *The broad direction you will take.*

7. The major targets it is trying to reach. *The major targets you are trying to reach.*

8. Guidelines of how capital and people resources will be employed. *Guidelines for your personal and capital resources.*

9. The culture under which it will operate. *The environment in which you want to operate.*

10. A view of itself. *Your view of yourself.*

11. A broad indication of production techniques and/or technology. *Your view of your skills and competencies.*

12. The public impression the organization will set forth. *How you want to be perceived.*

13. A clear indication of how the organization will relate to various stakeholders: customers, employees, stockholders, vendors, the community, government, and others.

How you will relate to the stakeholders in your life: family, friends, employees, bosses, fellow students, and others.

When you have worked out your mission statement, move on to firmly establish your goals. Do they relate to your mission? Do your goals and mission work together? These reworked goals should be firm and not changed easily. Remember the Never Ending Planning Cycle in Chapter 5? It illustrated that planning is a circular process and that you have to work back and forth around the circle as each step affects the other—planning is not a linear process.

DEFINITIONS

For clarity, let me give you my definitions of goals, objectives, strategies, and tactics:

Goals are the long-range aims or end aims that you want to reach. Some people will use the term *objectives* interchangeably with goals. For me, however, there is a difference.

Objectives are short-range aims. They have a shorter horizon than a goal, but a longer horizon than a tactic.

Strategies are how you will go about achieving your goals or end aims.

Tactics are devices used to accomplish an immediate specific end.

Definitions are aids and not important as long as you, and anyone you are sharing your planning with, understand the terms you use.

DEVELOPING STRATEGIES

The strategies you choose are the actions you will take to achieve your end aims or goals. Strategies, therefore, need to be developed for every goal you want to implement. You must use a strategy for whatever you do in order to achieve anything, consciously or unconsciously. For example, when you drive to work your goal is to arrive at a certain time. Your strategy is to take a particular route, one you probably drive each workday. If you hear on the radio that there's a traffic jam on your regular route, you will probably figure out an alternate route in order to achieve your goal of getting to work on time. You have gone from an unconscious strategy—how you usually get to work—to a conscious one—finding a better course of action to take.

Here are some points to keep in mind to establish the strategies for your goals:

- A series of "go/no-go" decisions is often required.

- More often than not, strategies involve unusual risk in the event of failure.

- Strategies are not just for major goals. They're needed for all aspects and at every level where actions are required.

- There is usually the need for a commitment for a long period of time.

- Strategies tend to change your purpose or direction.

- To develop a successful plan, all aspects of the process must be brought into full consciousness.

- Unusual benefits can be gained in the event of success.

- You must have a thorough understanding of the resources available in order to accomplish your strategies.

- You should plan on using maximum information.

- Your strategy should not automatically take the same path as past strategies.

When you work to develop your strategies, keep in mind that the actions you assign yourself must involve *doing the right thing, not doing the wrong thing right*. Too often we do a great job implementing the action, but we don't always select the right action. When you don't make a proper analysis or set the right goals, you can wind up having the right strategies for the wrong thing. That's why it is so important to go through the process carefully, diligently, thoroughly, honestly, and thoughtfully.

HOW TO USE
THE GOAL/STRATEGY FORM

The Goal/Strategy form illustrated on page 126 will help you develop your goals and strategies. It will also help you prioritize both your goals and strategies.

1. Use one form for each goal. Name the *Goal* on the line provided on the top left of the form. Leave the *Completion Date* blank for now.

2. Leave the *Rank* line, below the goal line, blank for now, too.

3. Once you have listed each goal on a separate form, list the rank you assign to that goal on the *Rank* line below the goal line.

4. For each goal, taking them in rank order— goal number 1, then number 2, and so on— list in the *Strategy* column your strategies—the actions you will take to accomplish that particular goal.

5. The next column *Person(s) Responsible* may or may not apply to your situation. If there is another person(s) who will be executing a strategy for you, put their name(s) in that column. Keep in mind that most of the strategies will have to be implemented by

you, so your name, more than any other, will appear in the column.

6. The *Date to be Accomplished* column is very important. If you don't set target dates to complete your strategies, you will have no way of measuring your progress toward successfully concluding the strategy and achieving your goal. It is also a guide to performing the actions you set for yourself in a timely manner.

7. The *What Will It Cost?* column is where you list any dollar, emotional, and energy costs. Nothing is for nothing. Everything has a cost. You should know the price you are paying to achieve each strategy and, thus, a goal.

8. List the benefit(s) or return(s) you anticipate from that strategy in the *Expected Return* column.

9. How will you know if you are successful in achieving your plan unless you have a means of monitoring and measuring your progress? In the *How to Measure* column, state how you will measure your progress in achieving that strategy.

10. When you've completed your list of strategies for the goal you have been working on, rank them in order of importance and put the rankings in the **RANK** column. At this time also enter the **COMPLETION DATE** of the goal on the same line as the goal at the top of the page.

Refer to the trigger questions later in this chapter for help if you are having trouble setting your goals and developing strategies. The Goal/Strategy form forces you to go through the process of answering the following questions:

- **WHAT:** What is your goal?

- **HOW:** What is your strategy?

- **WHO:** Who will do it?

- **WHEN:** What is the time frame?

- **INVESTMENT:** What will it cost in emotion, energy, and money?

- **WHY:** What is the expected return?

- **MEASURE:** Are you on the way to success?

Review your completed forms to see if these questions were answered when you filled them out.

FORM FOR DEVELOPING GOALS & STRATEGIES

GOAL _____

RANK _____

COMPLETION DATE _____

Strategy	Person(s) Responsible	Date to be Accomplished	What Will It Cost?	Expected Return	How to Measure	Rank

TRIGGER QUESTIONS TO HELP YOU SET YOUR FINAL GOAL

To help you to prepare your goals and strategies, here are some trigger questions:

- What would you like to achieve?

- How much would you like to earn in one, five, and ten years?

- How do you want to improve your health?

- Do you want to travel?

- Do you plan to be involved with church, politics, charities, sports, and/or other activities?

- What do you like to spend your time doing?

- Where do you want to live?

- What kind of environment do you want to be in?

- If you picture your life five and then ten years from now, what will it look like?

These are not dream questions, so try to be realistic in your answers. It's a good idea to go over them with a trusted friend who will be honest with you. What does your friend think of your answers? More important, what does he or she think about the goals and strategies you have worked out? My wife, always my trusted friend, helped me in every aspect of my life and planning. However, you need more than one friend's help. You need advisors and/or mentors who can augment the counsel of your dearest friend. Later in life, you should become a mentor to others. In mentoring, as in teaching, you learn a great deal from everyone you help.

HAVING MENTORS CAN ONLY HELP

When I started my business I looked for professional help: accountants, attorneys, and an advertising agency that would be honest advisors and grow with our company. At the time, I didn't think of them as mentors, with the exception of one person, our accountant Bob. I had always sought my Dad's counsel but I also sought advice, counsel, and professional accounting help from Bob. I was about 10 years old when I met Bob, who was a young man just starting his career. He was my Dad's accountant and came regularly to my Dad's hardware store on Staten Island to do the books. During those years we formed a bond.

When the United States entered the Second World War, Bob joined the army and soon became a major. When I joined the service, we corresponded and he was always available to offer advice. Upon returning to civilian life Bob earned a partnership in the accounting firm where he had been employed and eventually became the managing partner. Of course, he became our accountant and, to this day, forty years later, the firm still handles our accounting needs. His advice, through good and bad times, was tremendously helpful right from the start of our business. I would call Bob with every business problem, opportunity, or threat. He was always very honest in his analysis and did not spare my feelings—he was a good teacher.

Bob introduced us to our attorneys. I worked primarily with Avron and his associate. After forty years, they are still our attorneys, and not only good attorneys, but also good advisors. I never had quite the personal relationship with Avron that I have with Bob, but the relationship is a good and valued one.

When I was advertising manager for Dr. Posner Shoes, I met Al, a principal in Blaine Thompson advertising agency. He, too, proved to be a wonderful mentor. His advice was invaluable when we started our business and as we grew. I regret that I lost touch with him when he retired. These three people were the backbone of our unofficial advisory council. They helped me to plan and to think and to analyze my business and my life much more than they probably realize. Learning from them was a joyful experience because they gave of themselves, beyond fees, and were unselfishly interested in helping.

I believe in very long, if not lifetime, friendships. I also believe in the help you can get if you choose the right people as your advisors, mentors, and counselors. They offer valuable input into your life's planning and career.

MONITORING AND MEASURING

Monitoring and measuring are key factors to ensure that your plan is on track. Monitoring should be ongoing and brought to consciousness for virtually every action you take. In other words, keep your plan in mind at all times. Measuring, which involves analyzing your progress to see how much progress you are making, should be done at regular intervals. Once or twice a year is usually sufficient.

To measure my progress, I set or reset my plan on January first. I measure my progress again around June first. In my younger days, I would look at (monitor) my plan weekly. I kept it in my night table drawer and could not resist constantly checking to see if my actions that week contributed to implementing my plan or if I was getting off track. Over time, as I gained more experience in planning and working on my plan, I only needed to check it twice a year. I would, however, review and, if necessary, revise my plan if a major event seemed to affect it. When that happened, a minor adjustment was often all that was needed. Other times, a major change might be called for.

This happened to me; it might to you, too. One particular year my plan included the goal of "spending more time with my family." But we had a reversal in our business and lost the representation of our biggest factory. This was a severe loss. I had no choice but to augment my business activities with outside income. Not only did I have to postpone the goal of spending more time with my family, I had to change my business goals to deal with the drastic turndown. Fortunately I was able to cope with this business turndown by acting as sales manager for one of the other manufacturers we represented. This meant working seven days a week, ten hours a day, for at least a year. My wife understood the situation, and although she didn't like it, she accepted it and encouraged me. Our son was twelve years old at the time and I have always regretted that I did not have more time for him at this critical age. So I re-planned. One good thing that came out of this reversal of fortune was the realization that we had to adjust our business plan so that we would never again allow more than 25 percent of our income to come from a single manufacturer. We succeeded in this new business goal by finding new manufacturers to represent whenever any one of them started to produce 25 percent of our gross income. It took about a year to develop the business back up and for me to be able to implement my goal of spending more time with my family.

Monitoring is like checking the map to make sure you are on course to your destination. Measuring must be done at least once a year or whenever something occurs to change circumstances that will affect your plan. Time intervals for measuring are generally determined by the nature of the goal. To measure your progress ask yourself the following questions:

- Are you meeting the time targets?

- Are you on budget for your investments of emotion, energy, and money?

- Are projected results happening as planned?

- Is your attitude toward your goals still enthusiastic?

- Are your goals still consistent with your vision and mission?

- How close are you to achieving the goals?

- After re-reviewing the expected return, can you still anticipate the same or a better return, or are you off target?

- How do actual results compare to expected results?

TACTICS

I defined tactics as a device for accomplishing an immediate and specific end. Tactics are what battle-field noncoms use in order to implement their commander's strategies. An example in civilian life is a salesperson who has a goal to increase sales. If you were that salesperson, you would probably analyze your customers to determine the best strategies to accomplish the increase. As one of the strategies, you might establish spending more time with the 20 percent of the customers who give you 80 percent of your business. Then you might develop other strategies that would spell out how often to see each of your customers and who you would spend time with within the customer's organization (decision makers). You might have a strategy for increasing their volume by providing specialized services for them. The tactics you would use might include making a computer-based presentation to the buyer, offering to train the buyer's salespeople, and, perhaps, taking the buyer to a ball game or the theater to discuss your proposition in an informal atmosphere. These are all tactics to help your strategies become successful and to achieve your goal.

You will most certainly need to develop tactics to achieve your goals. In your daily activities, be aware of the tactics you will need to implement your strategies.

PRIORITIZE, PRIORITIZE, PRIORITIZE

The goals and strategies you choose, the priorities you set for them, and your sustaining priorities determine where you put your resources, what your emphasis will be, and, ultimately, dictate your direction in life. All of us have limited time and resources. As much as we might want to take in the world, the reality is that we can only take a bite at a time. Instead of taking bites at random, it's a good idea to do it systematically. Go after what is most important to you.

I am sure you sometimes have conflicting goals. For example, you might want to buy a summer house; you might also want to travel abroad. If you don't have the resources to do both, you must make a choice. Should you buy the house, knowing that the money required for mortgage and upkeep will keep you from traveling abroad for many years, or should you travel abroad while you're young and buy that summer house a number of years later? You have to prioritize one goal over the other.

In your planning, it is almost never possible to implement every goal at the same time. Establish priorities and time frames for achieving your goals. The importance of time frames will become apparent to you in Chapter 7.

7

PUTTING THE PLAN TOGETHER

*Things alter for the worse spontaneously if they
be not altered designedly. Therefore, he that
will not apply new remedies must expect new evils;
for time is the greatest innovator.*

—Francis Bacon, *Essays,* "Of Innovations" (1597)

Has this ever happened to you? You dream and
think about what you want to have happen in your life,
but reality sets in and you realize that it can never be.

FACING REALITY

I can recall when I dreamt and thought that I could
build a small business empire to pass on to my family. I

believed that if I could build one business, I could add another and then another. Our core business was Bobrow Sales Associates, Inc. Ten years later, we founded Bobrow Consulting Group, Inc. As the two companies grew, we added a vice president to the consulting company with the hope of building it into a multi-person organization. About that time we acquired a sales rep agency in the automotive aftermarket. Tom, one of the principals, became our partner and operating head of the automotive company. We also entered into a joint venture with another rep agency in a contiguous territory. This company was an attempt to expand our successful rep businesses into new territories. It was all well-planned and made a great deal of sense at the time. But it didn't work.

The main reason it failed was that we were not realistic about the time and energy we could give to each of these new entities. We thought we could easily transfer our reputation and success from Bobrow Sales to the other companies. After all, we had the infrastructure, the experience, and the knowledge. We found, however, that we were missing several ingredients. I believe the critical ingredient was my refusal to recognize that my arthritis, the pain it produced, and four back surgeries diminished my physical and psychic capacity to drive any new ventures. The new companies needed full-time attention; my diminished capacity did not allow me to provide the necessary leadership and drive. The operation of Bobrow Sales fell more and more on my brother's shoulders. As that company was our bread and butter, he had to spend the maximum amount of time with the company that paid the bills.

We relied on others to drive the new ventures. The result was that we failed to turn the automotive sales agency into a paying business. Also, it turned out that Tom wanted to take over the company for himself. Since my brother and I were not 100 percent active in the company, Tom was able to take over—we had to sell our shares to Tom at a loss. Things worked out a little better with the joint venture into contiguous territories. But again, it was not what we had planned—our plans were rather grandiose for the markets we were in. Because of our good relations with our partner, Harvey, we were able to buy the lines he had in our territory and he bought the lines we had in his. It was not a complete loss, although we did have to dissolve the company. We continued to cooperate with each other and enjoyed and profited from our ad hoc relationship.

The consulting company could not support our expansion plans, through no fault of our vice president, but because of my inability to physically go out and obtain business. At that point we decided that it was best for me to operate the consulting business on a solo basis and to continue my role of administering the sales agency and real estate interests we held.

I finally came to realize my limitations and what I could and could not do. The reality of my chronic illness had finally sunk in. I had to re-plan my goals, strategies, activities, and even my vision of the future. We also had to re-plan our business activities.

If you haven't already faced times when reality imposes itself upon your plan, you most likely will. I hope it will not be because of illness but, as we know, bad stuff happens. That's why it's a good idea to be alert to reality dictating changes to your plans.

Too often people develop grand plans but neglect to tie them to their resources. To avoid being unrealistic, pause for reality checks early on in the planning process, as well as throughout the process. Keep asking yourself the following questions:

- What are the dollars and time I can afford to risk in pursuit of my plan?

- Do I have the talents required?

- Have I the necessary skills or can I learn them?

- Have I the fortitude to stick to the plan?

- Have I researched my assumptions?

- Is there any other research I can do to be sure I'm being realistic?

- Do I have the overall ability to make the plan successful?

- Am I planning this because I have to prove I can do it or because I really want it?

- Am I in denial?

- Am I making reasonable assumptions based on logical analysis or only on hopes and dreams?

Do those with whom I share my plans think I'm being realistic?

Don't do as I did! Only move ahead with plans that you have the personal resources to implement; don't move ahead to prove you can do it.

CONTINGENCY PLANNING

Plans only deal with what you expect to happen. But, no matter how well you plan, the unexpected can and often will occur. Sometimes the unexpected is a favorable event, other times it is unfavorable. Always plan for the unexpected. What will you do if this strategy does not work out? What will you do if that goal cannot be achieved? Of course, you can't develop contingency plans for everything you undertake. You can, however, figure out what to do if a major goal falters. For example, if you are planning to become a doctor and you can't get into medical school or if you can't raise the money necessary to pay for your schooling, what will you do? If you are switching jobs and the new job falls through, what do you do? I know it isn't pleasant to think about failing to achieve a major goal, but you have to be prepared.

If contingency planning doesn't seem obvious to you, here are some of the benefits the process brings:

- It makes you aware of how unpredictable the future can be.

- It helps you to not think in absolutes.

- If you expect the unexpected, you are less likely to panic and more likely to react strategically.

- It puts you in a position to take advantage of unexpected opportunities.

- It prepares you to react to potential threats that become reality.

Although you can't have contingency plans for everything, you need to develop or build contingencies into your plans for major areas. Here are some things you can do to prepare:

1. Establish caution signs to watch for that will trigger planned reactions.

2. Estimate the benefit or harm that can happen should certain events take place. This will help you determine the major areas in which to establish contingency plans.

3. Be sure that whatever contingency plans you develop are true to your vision and mission.

4. Set up ways to monitor for the unexpected.

5. Develop action plans for key events that may occur.

You had better start worrying if you don't know what you would do if something you planned for did or did not happen.

You can help yourself think in terms of the probability of your plans working out if you develop a scenario for the following results:

1. **The most likely:** What do you think will actually happen?

2. **The least likely:** What is the worse-case scenario you can imagine for what you are planning?

3. **The most optimistic:** What is the best outcome you think can happen if everything goes beyond your expectations?

Do You Set Strategies First or Analyze First?

Set your strategies from your goals. But you must also set them from assumptions you make and from careful analysis. It is a process of moving back and forth. Some people will do it one way, some another. Whichever way you go about it, you still have to work back and forth to set, analyze, reset, and analyze until you are satisfied with what you have.

Since planning deals with an unknown future, we must make assumptions. You will make decisions based on these assumptions. An analysis of your *Strengths, Weaknesses, Opportunities,* and *Threats (SWOT)* will help you make more reasonable assumptions. The SWOT analysis is discussed later in this chapter. If assumptions are not as realistic as humanly possible, they may lead to a plan with false premises.

Here are some areas you may have to make assumptions for:

- Economic developments—personal, domestic, and global
- Your future financial situation
- Resources available
- Government regulations, restrictions, and actions that might impact your plan
- The impact of taxes
- Potential within your fields of interest
- Time to complete your goals

The planning process is essential and plans are vital in your personal life. When you consciously plan, you take your destiny into your own hands instead of relying on your unconscious to direct your life. If you don't bring your unconscious thoughts to the surface and examine them in the light of logic, they may remain buried within you as unrealized dreams. Write down your plan; it forces you to clearly think through what you are doing. Without a written plan, your mind can play tricks on you. You can forget some of your goals and strategies, or worse, distort them. There is nothing I recommend more strongly than to write out the planning process and the plan.

Most people start by listing strategies for their goals. After this list is completed, review the strategies by checking your assumptions. This is my preferred way. But whatever works for you is OK. The main reason to do this review is that you set out what you want your goals and strategies to be. Then you must relate them to what will work in the real world.

There are some obvious and some not-so-obvious situations that trigger re-planning. Here are a few that often occur:

- Change in your personal needs
- Major changes in the marketplace
- A new threat or opportunity due to a change in the economy
- Competition
- Financial problems
- Goals or strategies that don't seem to be working

- Illness
- Technological changes that may obsolete current strategies or offer new opportunities

USE A SWOT TO CHECK POSSIBILITIES FOR SUCCESS

It is one thing to develop your goals and strategies, it is quite another to look into the possibilities for achieving them. One of the keys to examine the assumptions you make is through research. Research means talking with people about your ideas and finding out how things really work—not relying on how you think they might work. In general, gather specific information that relates to each of your assumptions, goals, and strategies.

I know a young woman who, in her sophomore year at college, was thinking about career paths. She was leaning toward becoming an attorney, but was not sure she would like interacting with the volume of people that she believed all attorneys interact with. A solitary, studious person who was great at school, she liked to work by herself and did not have particularly good people skills.

When I asked her why she wanted to be an attorney, she said she had a passion for the law and that she thought it would be intellectually challenging. I then asked her if she had researched the kind of jobs attorneys pursue. She hadn't. I asked if she knew about constitutional lawyers and what was involved in pursuing that aspect of the law. Again she said no. I pried a bit more to find out if she had ever researched what was actually involved in the practice of law. Again she said no. I pointed out that she had to do some research to find out what lawyers really do, what types of practices there are, and whether or not all legal work involves a great deal of interaction with people. I further suggested she get in touch with the Bar Association, a law school, and a large law firm. After she had spoken with these people, she would have a realistic idea of what was involved in the study and practice of law.

It was important that she not make her decision based on TV and movie images or any prejudices she might have regarding the practice of law. She needed facts. I then suggested that she work up a list of questions she would like answered. I suggested she do some research in the library and on the Internet to find answers to her questions or add questions to her list before she met with anyone. I referred her to *Bacon's Publicity Checker,* a reference guide for magazines and newspapers, for the names of law journals and other publications dealing with law. After the research was concluded, she would be well prepared to ask intelligent questions and meet with people in and related to the profession. It is my experience that people are very willing to help when properly asked. She loved the idea of doing the research and it only took a few phone calls before someone she had targeted to talk with agreed to meet with her.

A SWOT is an analytical tool used for strategic planning. The acronym stands for Strengths, Weaknesses, Opportunities, and Threats. Use this same analytical tool to check your plan before putting it together. You have already analyzed your strengths and weaknesses. Now analyze the opportunities and threats that you might encounter in the implementation of your plan. Find out whether there are ample opportunities in the real world to accomplish your goals. What are they? How do they impact your plan? Look at the threats that may create interference.

When I chose to go into the independent sales rep agency business, I did not analyze what the earning potential might be in the hardgoods, hardware, or home improvement fields. I didn't research whether the same degree of effort to sell softgoods might produce a greater return for the time and effort expended than to sell hardgoods. Perhaps selling industrial products might have given an even greater return— perhaps not. The point is that I did not bother to research the potential of the field within which we chose to develop our business. Today, I would certainly look at potential before I entered any new field. Be sure to research the benefits of the choices you make.

Here are some questions to ask yourself:

- What advantage do I have over anyone else who may be competing with me?
- What can I offer that others can't?
- Do I have competition?
- From whom do I have competition?
- Are the opportunities within my abilities and resources?
- Can the threats be overcome?
- Are the threats worth overcoming?
- Is the risk factor worth the success it will produce?
- On balance, what are the odds that I will be successful?

You can use a simple chart, such as the one shown on the next page, to re-list your strengths and weaknesses and then add to your list of opportunities and threats. A chart will give you a visual comparison of these four factors and how they relate to each other to better analyze the impact they will have on your plan.

STRENGTHS	WEAKNESSES
You should have these from having previously done this analysis.	
OPPORTUNITIES	**THREATS**
List opportunities you can take advantage of.	List the threats you think may interfere with your plan.

SWOT worksheet

WHAT'S THE PAYBACK WHEN YOU SUCCEED?

Yesterday, June 3, 1998, I went to the graduation of Isabelle Duvernois, my future daughter-in-law, at Hunter College in New York. Isabelle is a great example of someone with a dream who set goals for herself and, with great persistence, hard work, and diligence, achieved her plan. I could not be more proud of her if she were my own daughter.

Isabelle emigrated from France to the United States about ten years ago. She had little or no money, but had high hopes and ambition. She did not speak our language but, as a trained actor, singer, and dancer, started to make the rounds while learning to speak English. She had to survive, so she took just about any job she could to support herself, mostly working in restaurants. Isabelle answered many audition calls and started to work in road shows and cabarets. This was her work for about six years. When she had enough of traveling and living out of a suitcase, she decided to pursue her passion, art restoration and art history. Isabelle got a job with Sony and enrolled in Hunter College, part of the City University of New York. She attended all classes and studied at night while holding a full-time day job. She carried a full-time program at school, just as a day student would. Since Isabelle's family in France could not help her, she had to make her way strictly on what she could earn and with the help of student loans. Isabelle had a plan; nothing within her control was going to stop her.

I knew Isabelle was in the honors program, which is even more difficult and demanding than the regular degree program. What I didn't know, until

graduation day, was that she had earned a near perfect 3.98 grade point average. Upon graduation, she
earned four scholarships and awards for academic
achievement. Isabelle now wants to earn a masters
degree in preparation for a career in art restoration.
It will not be easy. When she is married, she will still
have to work, continue her apprentice program with
an art restorer, and undertake new studies. Isabelle,
like many émigrés before her and the many yet to
come, worked very hard and made her own way
without anyone handing her anything or helping
her. She hit the big payoff—she realized her goal, a
Bachelor of Arts degree with highest honors.

When you have achieved what you set out to do,
the payoff is emotionally exhilarating and rewarding.
It makes you feel wonderful, builds your self-confidence, and raises your status in the eyes of others.
You walk away with the prize in hand for having at-
tained your goals. Cheers for Isabelle and all the
Isabelles who are making it happen for themselves!

WHEN DO YOU WANT IT TO HAPPEN?

It's all well and good to have plans, but plans must be
turned into action. By assigning specific times for
certain things to happen, a plan is moved from paper
to reality. Schedule completion dates to set the stage
for when various actions have to take place. The

schedule can be as simple as putting dates in your calendar or as complex as formulated diagrams, charts, and tracking devices. There are a number of computer programs to help you with your scheduling and tracking but, for personal planning, I don't think they are necessary. However, just in case you are dedicated to doing everything by computer, look into the following programs:

Fast Track Schedule 4.0
AEC Software, Inc.
Sterling, VA 20166
Phone: 703-450-1980
Fax: 703-450-9786
http://www.aecsoft.com

Plan & Track
Mainstay
591-A Constitution Ave.
Carmarillo, CA 93012
Phone: 805-484-9400
Fax: 805-484-9428
e-mail: Mainstay1@aol.com

Microsoft Project 4.0
1 Microsoft Way
Redmond, WA 98052
Phone: 800-426-9400 ext. 4-0619
http://www.microsoft.com

If you don't know when you want to achieve your goals and strategies, you can spend your whole life searching to complete them. While some goals and strategies are ongoing, most will and should have a completion date. When you develop your schedule, it is most important to call out the key events or milestones. They are the ones against which you will measure your progress. Milestones are measurable important events along the path to the fulfillment of your plan. For whatever you plan, there are always pivotal events you must make happen in order to move ahead. These milestones or key events will measure the achievement of your goals. If you have been working along with my suggestions, you have a clear list of your goals.

To develop your milestones for your schedule, consider the following:

- If you used the form in Chapter 6, you have indicated a completion date for your goal and completion dates for each of your strategies. From the completion dates for your strategies, assign milestone dates when the most important strategies are to be completed. Of course, it is a milestone when you have completed a goal.

- Develop a list of all the individual tasks that need to be done to accomplish the milestones. As is said, "the devil is in the details."

- Graph the information to make it easy to see and monitor.

If you prefer, put the dates in your calendar to make a simple Time and Activity Chart, similar to the example on the next page. It will help you break each strategy into tasks and assign a completion time for each task. You can develop the same kind of chart for your strategies, even for your tasks. The Time and Activity Chart will vary depending upon the complexity of your plan.

A Bar Chart, shown on page 155, is a little more complicated but much more graphic. It gives you a picture of how you are progressing toward the completion of your plan. It shows each task in relation to one another. Bar charts are often called Gantt charts.

The clear horizontal bar represents progress made for that activity; the solid black bar indicates the target completion month. At a six-month review, indicated by the dotted vertical line, we can see the progress made for each activity based upon a twelve-month time cycle. It shows that Task 1 is completed on time. Task 2 is completed ahead of time and Task 3 has five months for completion.

TASKS & MILESTONES	MONTHS											
	1	2	3	4	5	6	7	8	9	10	11	12
Develop Your Plan												
Develop your vision	●											
Draw up the mission		●										
Establish goals			●									
Set strategies			●									
Do SWOT analysis					●							
Review goals and strategies in light of SWOT						●						
Complete written plan								●				

Time and Activity Chart

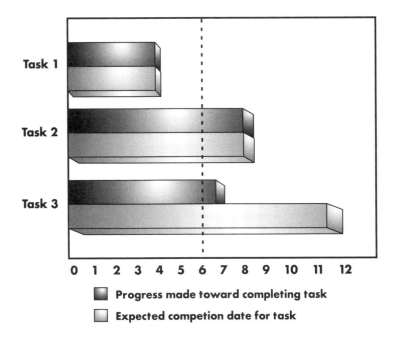

Task 1
Task 2
Task 3

0 1 2 3 4 5 6 7 8 9 10 11 12

Progress made toward completing task
Expected competion date for task

ASSEMBLING THE PLAN

The various elements of a plan must come together just as your five fingers do to make a fist. When they work together, they strike your goals or objectives with impact. To achieve this impact, you not only have to know what you're planning, you also need to know yourself. To know who you are and what you are planning is called strategic management; it marshals your resources to accomplish your goals. *Strategic management* is a process aimed at keeping your resources matched to the environments in which you operate.

All the elements will have to come together to form the written document—your plan. In previous chapters we spoke about developing your vision, mission, goals, and strategies. We also spoke about utilizing a SWLD, and in this chapter, a SWOT as an analytical tool. Now it is time to talk about the physical characteristics of your plan.

What form should your plan take to get the best results for you? No one can really say. Some people like "big" plans. Others like as brief a plan as possible. Whatever form you decide is best for you, be sure it is in writing. It should be what you find most comfortable to work with. Personally, I prefer short plans using as few pieces of paper as possible. I don't believe personal plans need a lot of detail. You may have produced many worksheets, but the plan itself should be a distillation of all your worksheets.

My plan has only three sheets of paper. It starts with my vision and my mission. I take each goal and its strategies from my worksheets and list them along with my target date for completion. It's simple, easy to review, and even easy to keep in your briefcase or pocket. The chart on the next page is an illustration of what it might look like. Some of you will want to bind each separate worksheet into a book, along with a summary page; that will become your plan.

VISION STATEMENT
MISSION STATEMENT

GOAL #1

Strategy #1   Date to be completed

Strategy #2   Date to be completed

Strategy #3   Date to be completed

And each additional strategy for Goal #1

GOAL #2

Strategy #1   Date to be completed

Strategy #2   Date to be completed

Strategy #3   Date to be completed

And each additional strategy for Goal #2

GOAL #3

Strategy #1   Date to be completed

Strategy #2   Date to be completed

Strategy #3   Date to be completed

And each additional strategy for Goal #3

Plus as many goals and strategies that you have

A Graphic Outline of My Plan

BUILDING THE PLAN

There are other forms your plan can take. Here are some thoughts on how you might want to keep your personal plan:

- A three-ring binder, with clearly delineated sections can be a very good method. All your worksheets can be in a work section, research in another, and the final plan in another.

- A diary or bound workbook, which would include all your working and collateral documentation.

- An unbound short plan that might resemble mine on the previous page.

- Each section bound separately in modules so that the modules can be included or excluded.

- Whichever way you find most helpful.

As a review, here are the elements you should have worked through to arrive at your written document—the plan.

1. **Your vision:** What you envision your plan will ultimately achieve.

2. **Your mission:** What you are setting forth to do.

3. **Clear goals:** Your end aims.

4. **Your strategies:** How you want to achieve the end aims.

5. **Who will do it:** Some things may require others to do something for you in relation to your plan.

6. **When will it be done:** Schedule with milestones.

7. **What will it cost:** Energy, dollars, and emotion.

8. **Your expected results:** What you will get for investing your time and money.

9. **What success will be:** Your own definition of success.

10. **Method for monitoring and measuring results:** The method you have chosen.

WHAT IF YOU DON'T LIKE PLANNING?

When I asked my brother whether he saw himself as a success, he immediately answered, "Of course I am. Look at the money I make. Look at the business my partner and I have built." He then asked, "You mean in business?" I said, "No, not just business, but in life." He thought a moment and said, "Yes, I think I am. I have a caring wife and two wonderful daughters. I enjoy the work I do and my involvement with the Masons. I will feel even more successful, though, when my two daughters are happily married and settled down with their own families. I do feel generally successful in my life." My brother, who I think is very successful in all aspects of his life, would not develop a plan as I advocate. He tells me that he does plan—it's in his head. I know he does that. I also feel that if a crisis developed in his life, he would think differently and go through the planning process.

There have been a number of people to whom I have suggested my planning method and who said they would do it, but somehow, never did get around to it until they were in crisis. I can think of at least six people who have told me that for the longest time they didn't think it necessary to go through the steps I outlined and to write down their plan. For each of them, a time did come when they became stuck in their lives. They each tried my method and were amazed at how helpful it was. They all said it set them on new paths in their lives. One young friend told me that he did his planning with his wife. He felt they both needed to figure out, together, what they wanted to do with the rest of their lives.

I have been around long enough to realize that many of you will not go through the process I advocate, no matter how hard I try to convince you of its value. For those of you who will not plan as thoroughly and methodically as I advocate, I hope you will at least plan in whatever way you are comfortable and that it proves helpful to you.

Part III

But, It Takes Much More Than a Plan

Learn how to successfully implement your plan.

8

HOW TO GET INSIDE YOURSELF

*I saw the moment, and I took advantage
of the moment. I never doubted myself.*

—Michael Jordan of the Chicago Bulls, as reported in the *New York Times,* June 15, 1998, after sinking the winning basket to clinch the NBA championship the day before.

Have you ever felt like this: conflicted, down in the dumps, not sure what work you should do, unsure of how to relate to people, wanting to do what your body tells you not to do—in general, just messed up in your head? Well, I have. Let me tell you what I did to help put myself back on the path to success.

Throughout most of his life, my Dad suffered from arthritis of the spine. I undoubtedly inherited his genes.

A short time after he died in 1982, I visited the New York chapter of the Arthritis Foundation, made a donation in his memory, and volunteered to help in their work. I soon became a member of their Board of Governors and, later, a member of the Executive Committee and a vice president. Although I was honoring my Dad's memory, it didn't take me long to realize how therapeutic this volunteer work was for me. I was recuperating from what happily proved to be the last of my back surgeries; mentally, I was a mess. I had not yet learned how to manage my pain. I hadn't yet realized that I needed to be with other people with arthritis and to feel that I was able to help others. I joined an arthritis support group; served on the national committee for their new magazine *Arthritis Today;* helped establish a thrift shop in Manhattan; and did pro bono consulting that helped the New York chapter develop their first strategic plan.

The Arthritis Foundation consists of a group of caring individuals. Their competent president and chief executive officer is a fine human being and the driving force of the New York chapter. He and their chief operating officer are always available and helpful. Everyone in this organizations is capable, kind, gentle, considerate, helpful, and dedicated to the cause— a joy to work with. However, I was sometimes a problem for them. My pain often overcame me and I became short-tempered and intolerant. They always understood and worked with me. Now I am a member of the Board of Governors Emeritus, still close to the foundation, and happy whenever they call and ask for my involvement.

Years later, when I developed prostate cancer, I thought that what had helped me adjust to my arthritis would also help me adjust to my feelings about having cancer and my treatment. I volunteered my services to the American Cancer Society, Manhattan Unit, and I was asked to join their Board of Directors. My experience with this organization was not as helpful or as rewarding as my involvement with the Arthritis Foundation. Although the other volunteers were admirable people, the professional staff and their method of working with and utilizing volunteers left me cold. My involvement did result in something positive: I met a volunteer who, along with her husband, became good friends. In addition, my work with the American Cancer Society helped me learn from other cancer survivors and understand what was happening to me.

My plan had been to achieve some specific successes in order to feel useful again and to get rid of the muddle in my mind. I felt certain that if I became more involved in business, writing, teaching, and other activities, I would get myself straightened out. These activities all helped, but no one activity was the solution I was looking for—I was still muddled. I realized that I had to address all aspects of my needs to turn the situation around. I realized that I needed to exercise, work on creative projects, and engage in business activities with clients as well as other planned activities. I learned to periodically rest my body during the day. I still traveled internationally to visit with business clients and for pleasure, but I paced myself. Whenever I was delayed in an airport, I was not embarrassed to find a bench to lie down on or even to use the floor if necessary. Whenever I anticipated a strenuous day of travel, I would leave the following day free to rest. Although these were major adjustments, I was able to accomplish them. More important, they worked.

IT'S MESSY IN THERE

Self-reverence, self-knowledge, self-control,
These three alone lead life
to sovereign power.

—Alfred, Lord Tennyson, "Oenone," (1832), l.142

Getting inside ourselves is difficult enough, nevermind figuring out what we want and what success will be at any particular time. Sometimes you feel as if the mess within will never let you come back into balance. Often that's when you need professional help. I certainly felt that way during the time I was wrestling with accepting what I could not change—my arthritis. Involvement with the Arthritis Foundation helped, but it didn't resolve my conflicts. After all, that was only one part of my life. More was needed to straighten myself out. As my surgeon reminded me, "The mind is an organ, too." I learned that I needed help in making the adjustment to a chronic condition.

I spoke to my cousin who is a doctor and a friend. A scientist with a heart, he is the kind of physician who never takes away hope. His philosophy is that if one doctor can't help you, keep searching until you find a doctor who can. He recommended a psychiatrist he thought could help me, and I began therapy. The psychiatrist taught me how to manage my pain and helped me accept and work with my limitations. He also helped me realize that only I could straighten myself out. He couldn't do it, pills couldn't do it— no one could, but me. My wife was supportive and understanding, which proved a major source of comfort and help. Others helped as well but, in the final analysis, it was up to me.

If you feel messed up inside, here are some things I learned that help during difficult times:

- First, stop resisting, denying, or fighting reality. I don't mean that you should accept being out of balance and feeling confused for the rest of your life; what I do mean is to accept who you are at this moment and trust your ability to build a better situation that will move you past your confusion and toward clear directions.

- I learned that you should go with what you have and what you are capable of doing. It will likely turn out that you can do much more than you think.

- I take twenty or thirty minutes, usually in the middle of the day, to quiet myself and practice meditation. It's time set aside for going into myself and puts me in a more relaxed state of mind. Sometimes I even fall asleep for fifteen minutes or so. It doesn't help every time, but most of the time it does.

- Deep breathing along with meditation helps relax body muscles. It's easy—just take a deep breath and, as you exhale, slowly direct the breath into the area of your body that is most painful and tense. "Think it" into the area. It takes a little time to get the knack but, when you do, you will find it a very relaxing technique.

- If you feel you can't do it yourself, get help from a professional.

- Physical activity is extremely important, even if it means just taking a few steps a day until you can build yourself up. Physical activity helped me kick all the pain medication I was taking. As a young man I had worked out aggressively, playing four-wall paddleball at a gym before health clubs became popular.

More recently, I underwent physical therapy and I now exercise regularly. I speed walk a couple of miles a day, do a regimen of floor exercises for thirty minutes twice a day (prescribed for my arthritis), and work out with light weights. This program releases tension and reduces pain. I exercise in a meditative, non-combative, non-aggressive manner. The small physical victories I achieved restored confidence in my physical self. It also helps keep me in balance physically and mentally. If you exercise consistently, it can help relieve tension, build a strong body, and mentally put you back on track.

- Attack when you feel good and retreat when you are under attack. In other words, try not to push yourself when you are feeling oppressed; make your moves when you are feeling good.

- Start to plan how you will improve your state of mind. Your main goal is to become the best that you are capable of.

- Be consistent and persistent without becoming a fanatic.

- Learn to listen to your body and your state of mind and follow their lead.

- Don't make major decisions when you're down or when you feel very up. If possible, make the major decisions in your life when you feel calm, strong, and in balance.

- Have a clear picture of what success will be for you.

There are all kinds of success. But without successfully straightening out the mess inside, other successes will not come easily.

GET TO KNOW YOURSELF

Whether you are going through a difficult period or sailing along according to plan, the better you know yourself the more likely you are to happily achieve your goals. Some of the exercises previously suggested, such as listing your strengths, weaknesses, likes, and dislikes (SWLD), will certainly help. But you can do more. Begin by not taking your behavior for granted. Explore why you do certain things in a particular way, think in certain patterns, and respond to situations as you do. Strive to know who and what you are and why you are a particular way. Start with wanting to know yourself and not taking on life in automatic drive.

Introspection does not mean you are egocentric—it is a healthy and useful tool toward success. To know what you want and what is important to you defines the parameters of life within which to set your goals. I recall talking with a student, let's call her Iris, who could not focus on her goals. Iris didn't know what success would be for her or what she really wanted to do with her life. All she knew was that she wanted everything and almost anything. Iris believed that money and fame would make her absolutely happy. On the surface, this sounds reasonable. Many people think that money solves everything and that fame brings happiness. Iris told me that if she had a lot of money, she could buy whatever she wanted and, if she had fame, she would feel wanted, loved, and worthy. Iris was chasing false gods. Don't get me wrong; it's great to have money—but money is not *the* source of happiness.

Money can give you freedom of choice, make you comfortable, and certainly helps when adversity strikes. In and of itself, however, money can't buy you happiness nor does recognition by others restore self-worth. Money cannot buy health or the life of a loved one lost, nor can money put you in balance. Self-worth and happiness are states of mind that come from how you perceive yourself and from satisfying your inner drives. I tried to explain all this to Iris, but it didn't seem to help her. It took a tragedy in her life, the loss of her brother—someone she loved very much—to cancer, to make her turn inward. At first Iris was devastated, then she mourned. She told me that something deep inside began to stir about six months after her personal tragedy. She started to see herself and the world differently.

Iris no longer wanted to acquire things or spend all her money, buying for the sake of buying or for the satisfaction of feeling important. Buying and acquiring became unimportant. Instead, she dedicated herself to helping people with cancer. Suddenly she knew what she wanted success to be, and it wasn't fame or earning money. Iris had found what was important to her. What she needed to be happy was to feel in balance and to feel successful—by having an impact on people and affecting their lives in a positive way. Iris now had clear goals: go to medical school, do charity work with cancer patients, eventually have a family, and build the kind of loving relationship and friendship with others that she had had with her brother.

It took a traumatic event to make Iris perceive herself and the world in a new way. She realized that, before her brother died, she had been filling her emptiness with a desire for things. She kept buying things to fill her emptiness and because it gave her a sense of power to be the buyer. Iris came to realize, however, that what she used to have were unrealistic Hollywood and TV dreams; she had no other dreams of substance.

When Iris began searching her inner self—her needs, wants, and desires—she figured out what was important to her and what made her feel happy, worthy, and self-satisfied. The terrible shock of losing her brother turned her inward. Don't wait for a tragedy in your life to propel you to examine your inner needs, wants, and desires. Examine them now. It will take some reflection and thought. Conversation with trusted friends also helps. Mainly, though, have an honest dialogue with your inner self.

To understand what you really want from life, you must always be conscious of the following:

- **What excites you?** Not what excites you just for the moment, but what consistently excites you whenever you come in contact with it. It might be music, art, problem solving, working with people—anything you always seem passionate about. Follow that passion.

- **What makes you feel alive and vibrant?** Feeling alive and vibrant means doing whatever makes you feel that way, whether you are anticipating, doing, or revisiting the action. Feeling alive and vibrant produces sustained satisfaction. When my wife or I get out of balance and are not feeling alive, we often feed our souls by visiting a museum, taking in a play, attending a concert, or just going out into the country and getting close to nature. For me, it also happens when I am engaged with a client, writing, teaching, or arbitrating a dispute. The important thing is to know what will do it for you.

- **What makes you totally unaware of time?** When I write, I get lost in time. This also happens when I'm seeing a movie or a play that absorbs me completely or when I am involved in problem solving.

- **What helps you relax?** For me, it's meditation, relaxation techniques, playing a sport, exercising, and, oh yes, watching "Star Trek" or "The X-Files."

- **When do you feel in balance?** None of us can feel in balance all the time. It's natural to go in and out of balance. I feel in balance when I'm involved in creating and problem solving. I usually go out of balance after the completion of a project until I find a new goal or begin another project. As I work on the new goal, I can go in and out of balance depending upon what's happening in my life. The successful completion of each aspect in the achievement of the goal tends to get me more in balance.

- **Don't expect to be in balance all the time.** Pay attention to what brings about balance for you. Work toward it without the despair of feeling out of sync.

- **What makes you happy?** That's a difficult question to answer. I wonder if any of us can easily define happiness. We recognize happiness, but can't always put into words what produces it. Getting to know the essence of yourself can help define what happiness is for you.

- **What gives you a sense of self-worth?** Many famous people lack self-worth. Self-worth comes from within, not from outside, ourselves. There are often times when something from the outside world triggers a feeling of self-worth, but even then, it is truly a reflection of how you feel about yourself. I believe that self-worth stems from the successful completion of whatever you set out to do.

- **What things leave you empty after completing them?** We all do thingsout of habit or because we feel we must, things that sometimes leave us feeling empty or depleted. This feeling is a sure sign to avoid these activities, if you possibly can, for they drain your energy and give you nothing in return. Usually this happens when you undertake a task or get involved with something you really didn't want to do. If you get no nourishment from doing something you wanted to do or feel empty afterward, examine why you wanted to do it in the first place.

- **Keeping a diary can be a big help in plotting your inner feelings and what triggers them.** The key is to write down how you feel day by day and what you think made you feel that way. Review what you have written to help get to know yourself better.

You must force your attention to how you feel when you are doing things or when you are involved in a particular project.

FOLLOW YOUR BLISS

The heading for this section is borrowed from Joseph Campbell and the ideas he expressed in his book *The Power of Myth* (Doubleday, 1988).

It's good to be just plain happy; it's a little better to know that you're happy; but to understand that you're happy and to know why and how...and still be happy, be happy in the being and the knowing, well that is beyond happiness, that is bliss.

—Henry Miller, *The Colossus of Maroussi,* (1941) pt.1

When the voices within you become clear, you are on your way to finding your bliss and knowing yourself. Bliss is to be at one with what we experience when we are totally into our work or play activity. We also feel bliss when we are deeply relating to another person, when we are in love, and when we fulfill a purpose, listen to our inner self, or follow our mission.

Bliss is the state of feeling totally in balance, deeply content, and living in the moment.

Here are some suggestions to help you follow your bliss:

- Make friends with your inner self. Study your inner self and come to understand your desires and joys.

- Learn how to get in touch with your inner self. Practice any technique you find that works for you—meditation, relaxation response, listening to music, whatever. Exercise the technique regularly. Don't let the vicissitudes of daily life take you away from reaching inside yourself.

- You are worthy of and have the right to embrace the things you personally love and enjoy. Seek whatever is pleasurable, whatever allows you to live in the moment.

- Money and power may be great to have, but they seldom bring you to a state of bliss. More often they produce agitation or excitement. Even if you are very materialistic, seek from within that which puts you in balance, makes you feel whole, unified, integrated—in short, produces a state of bliss.

- We all know that perception is in the eye of the beholder. You are the beholder; the realities of your life lie within your perception. Your perception is what makes sense of or relates the outer world to your inner world. Bliss will come through how you perceive. Consciously challenge your perceptions; those that are honest and good will usually make you feel blissful.

- Follow your LifePlan as a means of finding your bliss.

- The "doing" is where your bliss resides. Very often, when I look into my wife's eyes or when I hug my son and daughter-in-law, I find a deep sense of bliss. It often happens when I'm writing or involved in doing that which suspends time for me and makes me feel in balance.

- Accept that you will always be in the pursuit of bliss, that you will go in and out of bliss, and that you cannot sustain bliss. When you experience bliss, however, it is wonderful.

The psychologist Abraham Maslow studied the nature of human experience. He found that the moments when people were happiest, when they felt most accomplished and fulfilled—called a peak experience—occurred when they felt fully actualized, utilized their inner resources, and usually addressed a single activity as it occurred in a particular moment in time. He also found that, during the peak experience, you feel more of being yourself and merge with the activity you are involved in. Krishnamurti, a teacher who bridged the philosophies of the East with the West, taught that for true understanding and a full experience, the observer should become the observed. You have probably experienced this feeling: when listening to music, you seem to become the music; when looking at a beautiful sunset, you become the sunset. It is what the ancient Chinese described in the pursuit of Tao, the path that brings balance and bliss.

OPPORTUNITIES RESIDE IN CHAOS

> *Chaos often breeds life,*
> *when order breeds habit.*

—Henry Brooks Adams (1838–1918)
The Education of Henry Adams (1907), Ch. 13

The state of bliss is certainly good and desirable. But the place where things happen, things that tend to move us and that change the world, is at the edge of chaos and order. Just as we go in and out of bliss, we also go in and out of chaotic periods in our lives. This process takes place in our personal lives, in business, in professions, in economic and political systems, and in nature itself. Often, when we begin to come out of chaotic periods—when we are at the edge of chaos—new ideas, thoughts, ways of being, perceptions, and change take place. In nature, new forms, symmetry, and organizations of matter come out of the universal chaotic state.

For more on chaos and chaos theory, read *Making a New Science* by James Gleick (Penguin, 1988); *Complexity…The Emerging Science at the Edge of Order and Chaos* by Mitchell Waldrop (Touchstone Books, 1993); *At Home in the Universe* by Stuart Kauffman (Oxford University Press, 1996); and *Thriving on Chaos* by Tom Peters (HarperCollins, 1991).

You know the old saying—for every ending there is a beginning. Beginnings usually develop out of chaotic periods. When we are disturbed or out of balance—not in a state of bliss—we become most creative. When you're restless, don't know what you want to do, and feel somewhat desperate, trust that opportunity and change will develop. It's hard to hang onto trust when you're feeling chaotic, but hang on, you must.

Think back to times when you were mixed up, unsure, and didn't know what to do next. Didn't opportunities develop and change take place? Admittedly, the opportunities and the change are not always positive, but often they are. When you are in a chaotic period, stay aware; you will often find creativity within yourself. If you understand what's going on, by thoughtful planning you can direct your creative energies toward positive change.

I believe that everyone can be creative. Of course, it depends on how you define creativity. I don't mean that we all have the potential to paint a great picture, produce marvelous music, or invent something new. What I do mean is that we can all put something together that is new for us. It might be to whittle a toy, construct a simple table, knit a sweater, create a new business, develop a new way of doing a particular task—something new to you. Take the elements that already exist and put them together in a different way. This kind of creativity is heightened when it occurs on the edge of chaos.

I can recall how chaotic it felt when I changed my business activities and moved my office into my home. I wasn't sure which direction to head for, how to put together the resources I had, and, most of all, I was ambivalent about the work I wanted to do. Out of this state of chaos I was able to create a new mode for operating my consulting business, create a new course to give at New York University, and come up with an idea for a new book. After I got through the dark stage of uncertainty and confusion, my creative juices started to flow and I began to develop plans that would bring me about positive change in my life. Try to remember this: Whenever there is chaos, there is also opportunity.

TEN WAYS TO MAKE ORDER OUT OF CHAOS

The following list of ideas will help when life is chaotic and unbalanced.

1. Don't lose your head. Sometimes what is going on is so difficult that you want to run away or hide. At times you may become too paralyzed to act. That's when you have to believe, deep down, that you can make order out of chaos and even create new opportunities from the circumstances.

2. Keep telling yourself that you can make productive order out of your chaos. Make it a mantra; recite it over and over throughout the days of chaos.

3. It is important to develop a positive attitude and positive thinking. You will be surprised at how well this works.

4. Explore your dreams and vision of the future. They will tell you how you would like things to be. Be realistic about the dreams you choose to pursue.

5. If you could wave a magic wand and put things back in order, how would you do it? What would the new order look like?

6. Talk with your best friend, an advisor, your mentor, and any other people you trust. They can be a sounding board for your feelings and desires.

7. If you can't sort things out by yourself or with the help of people with whom you share your feelings, seek professional help.

8. Since you do not have that proverbial magic wand, you must be the one responsible to turn what you dream or envision into reality.

9. Start to convert your vision of the future into reality by initiating the planning process.

10. Give yourself time. There are no magic formulas that produce instant results.

It is vital to get inside yourself to become successful. If you don't understand yourself, know what you want, what your resources are, what your capabilities are, and if you haven't defined what success will be for you, it isn't likely that you will succeed. Get to know yourself. Plan, so that you are able to take advantage of whatever situation you're in, good or bad. It's a great way to become a success.

9

BREAKING PARADIGMS: OTHER WAYS OF SEEING

According to Webster's *Ninth New Collegiate Dictionary,* a paradigm is an example, a pattern; especially an outstandingly clear or typical example or archetype.

WHAT EXACTLY IS A PARADIGM ANYWAY?

Paradigms are habitual ways of seeing things, or always doing things by the same rules. It's a particular vision of reality. Paradigms establish boundaries and tell you how to behave within those boundaries. Paradigms prescribe your thinking. It's like thinking within a box. Breaking paradigms produces new ways of seeing and thinking, a new game with new rules, a shifting of focus and perception, and seeing in a different way. Breaking paradigms requires thinking out of the box.

Paradigm breakers are people who deal with problems in new ways. They change the rules of the game. Basketball, baseball, football, golf, and tennis are apt metaphors for paradigms. You play the games within defined areas—a court, a field, a course—and rules tell you how to play the game successfully. If you change the paradigm, it alters the rules of the game; if you change the rules, you change the paradigm.

In the June 28, 1998 edition of the Magazine Section of the *New York Times,* an advertisement run by The Montgomery Funds demonstrates how our paradigms tend to affect how we see and evaluate things. The ad showed two photos side by side. One showed an attic filled with old furniture and other stored items—the kind of junk we all tend to put in our attics, garages, or basements. Among the odds and ends was a painting propped up on an old chair. Under this photo was printed $25. In the photo next to it was a picture of a museum setting with the same painting hanging on the wall. A small plaque was next to the painting. In front of the painting, posts with velvet covered ropes prevented people from getting too close. Under this picture was printed $250,000. The copy that accompanied the two photographs read, "As Sherlock Holmes once remarked to Watson, 'You see, but you don't observe.' Which, in a rather cogent nutshell, is the problem most of us face in the world of investments." The ad then goes on to talk about investments.

This advertisement dramatically illustrates two different ways of seeing the same thing. I hope my description gets the impact across to you. This ad sets forth the major point of this chapter—there clearly are different ways of seeing. We must shift our paradigms in order to find the true value of what we look at.

Here is an example of how seeing things differently led to big profits. Around fifty years ago, my Dad and Mom bought a painting for $125. Dad saw it in the window of a small framing store and fell in love with it. When he took my Mom to see it, she felt as he did and wanted the painting. At that time, $125 was a lot of money and they debated whether they could afford it. They did buy it and hung it over their bed. It was a lovely painting of a woman with a kitten on her lap reclining on a chaise lounge.

After my Dad passed away and my Mom could no longer live in her home in Florida because of the progression of Alzheimer's disease, we brought her to New York to live in a nearby nursing home. She is now 91 years of age and still resides there. After she moved into the home, I went to Florida to close down her apartment. I called my brother, my mother's sister, and my wife to ask what they might like to have from the apartment. Some possessions were donated to charity and some went to the woman who had cared for my Mom in Florida. Neither my brother, nor his wife, nor my wife wanted to hang the painting in their homes. My wife said that although she might not hang the painting, it was too fine an oil painting to give away. So it was shipped home with the other things. When we unpacked it, my wife noted that it was painted at the end of the last century by someone named Skipworth, probably a British painter, and she felt the painting had artistic value. Gloria saw it very differently than I did. I saw it as a painting lovingly associated with my parents; she saw it as a work of art. Gloria shifted my habitual way of seeing the painting.

Gloria went to the Metropolitan Museum of Art's library to research the artist and discovered that Frank Markham Skipworth was a known painter of the late 1800s. In fact, he had been a member of the Royal Academy of Art in London where several of his paintings hung. We took a photo of the painting, sent it to Sotheby's (the auction house), and asked what they thought the painting (called "Teasing the Kitten" and painted in 1884) would bring at an auction. To our surprise, they said they would set a $10,000 reserve on it, which meant they would not accept a bid for less than $10,000 when auctioned. They also thought it should bring between $10,000 and $20,000. We decided to auction the painting.

My wife and I attended the auction and experienced some of the most exciting moments of our lives. When our painting came on the block, the opening bids were slow. I whispered that it looked like we wouldn't get a bid to meet the reserve fund requirement. Then we heard $10,000 called, a second later $20,000, and then $30,000. I could hardly catch my breath. All of a sudden the bidding was up to $40,000. In my excitement, I started to punch my wife in her arm and then, in a wink, the bidding escalated to $50,000, $60,000. The final bid was $80,000. The painting was sold, over the phone, to someone unknown to this day.

If Gloria had not seen the painting as a fine work of art, its real value would probably never have been discovered and the painting would have been lost to the art world. We, of course, would never have realized such a large profit, although, after taxes and fees to the auction house, we netted about half from the sale. Nevertheless, it helped support some of my mother's nursing home needs.

PARADIGM BREAKERS

Entergy Corporation, one of the largest electric utility companies in this U.S., was a client of ours. They now own electric companies in Arkansas, Texas, Louisiana, and Mississippi as well as in England, Australia, and South America. Back in 1989, when they were known as Middle South Utilities, we began consulting for them. A few months after we began our project, they changed their name to Entergy Corporation. The change of name signaled a major shift in the culture of the company. At the time of the change, they were facing the start of deregulation in the electric industry. They knew that the government would gradually change regulations that, in turn, would change the rules of the game for all electric utilities. Because they did not know exactly what the new rules would be, they wanted to prepare the company to face an uncertain future. They realized that no matter what the new regulations ultimately were, they would clearly have to offer new products and services. Our assignment was to help them to install a corporation-wide process for developing and marketing new products and services.

We found the people at Entergy typical of others in this industry: engineering-oriented people resistant to change. For years the company had been managed by these engineering types and driven by production and government regulations. A strong company culture that most of the executives were comfortable with existed and they did not want to see it changed. Whenever we suggested any changes, we were told: "We don't do things that way" or "We can't do that" or "We have never done it that way before." Other expressions also told us that what we were proposing was against the established rules of the game—the company paradigms. Our attempts to install the new product and services development process were hampered.

We worked with the team leader in charge of our project. Together we determined that a cultural change within the company was needed in order to develop and market new products and services successfully. John, who is very creative and a great manager, came up with a concept to bring about a paradigm shift: a Culture Buster program. We distributed Culture Buster tee shirts, coffee mugs, newsletters, many other devices, and a unique item for people who were part of our new products teams to keep on their desks. It was a spray bottle that shot out a mist of water, like a plant mister. The bottle was imprinted with the Culture Buster logo. When someone said, "We can't do that" or "We never did it that way before," we would let him or her have it with a mist of water from the Culture Buster spray bottle. It was a great joke. People joked about it; it became the talk of the executives; it brought dramatic attention to the need to change how people see and think. It didn't, by itself, magically change the company culture, but it did help us gain cooperation and acceptance for what we were trying to accomplish.

YOU BRING YOUR CULTURE WITH YOU

As with companies, so it is with individuals. We all have established ways of doing things, a culture in which we operate. Seeing differently, breaking paradigms, usually helps us see new opportunities. If we can develop the foresight that seeing things differently

can open to us, we can be on the cutting edge
of opportunity.

The most successful people break paradigms. They
are willing to see differently and change the game.
Bill Gates of Microsoft changed the game, as did
Thomas Edison and Henry Ford. They changed our
lives and, in so doing, changed their own lives. You
too, in your personal life, must develop ways of jog-
ging yourself into seeing differently and breaking
paradigms. If you say to yourself, "It can't be done,"
or "I never did it that way before," or "I can't do
that," or whatever rationalization you give for not
taking on something new or shifting the way you see
things, then you had better get a bottle of "paradigm
breaker" and spray yourself! You need to find ways
to look at things from many different perspectives.

THE YOUNG BEAUTY
AND THE OLD LADY

Here are some examples that may help you see differently. At the very least, they will illustrate different
ways of looking at things. In Joel Arthur Barker's
book *Paradigms: The Business of Discovering the Future*
(HarperCollins, 1992), the author gives the following
exercise. Here is a column of numbers based on 10.
Add them in your head as quickly as you can. Don't
use a pencil. Write the sum down.

1000
40
1000
30
1000
20
1000
10
_____

If your total is 5000, that is the answer that 95 percent of the people get when they add up the numbers. Add the numbers again. Now read the next paragraph for the correct answer and find out why you may have been wrong.

Barker tells us, "Now, the question is: Why do so many people arrive at 5,000 for their sum? The answer has to do with our confidence in our adding. Most of us add it right to 4,090 and then screw up completely carrying the 1. The correct answer is 4,100." If you were wrong, it was because your paradigm of how you see numbers took over and obscured the true solution.

Our fixed way of seeing often interferes with our problem solving. Here is a classic problem to illustrate why it is necessary to shift your paradigm in order to find solutions. Barker uses this example in his book as well.

Illustrated below is a square with four points, one in each corner. The challenge is to move only two dots and create a square twice as big. If you are having trouble solving the problem, here is a hint. Think of the square as a diamond. In other words, view it from any one of the points instead of head-on as a square. Look at the next illustration for the solution. You can then see the points to move to make a bigger box.

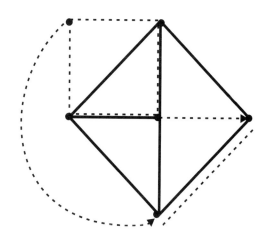

We are often so sure that we see clearly and correctly but, by shifting our view, we find there is more to what we are looking at. Gaze at the following illustration. What do you see, a young woman or an old woman?

If you keep looking at the picture, you will find one can change into the other, depending upon your perception. If you have trouble finding the old or young woman, first close one eye and then look at the picture with both eyes open, or slowly blink to shift your focus. It will come to you. You can do the same with the next illustration to shift your view of a vase to a silhouette of two figures facing one another, or vice versa.

Most of you are probably quite familiar with the examples I used to call your attention to different ways of seeing and perceiving. I purposely used them to focus your attention on the importance of being able to see things from different vantage points. Success is very much dependent on this ability.

*The most successful people are usually
the ones who can shift paradigms.*

HOW WE PERCEIVE THE PROBLEM MAY BE THE PROBLEM

While I was writing this book, Apple Computer ran a great advertising campaign. It showed the Apple logo with the following words under it: "Think Different." Apple often pictured individuals who are known for their success because they thought differently—Einstein, Edison, Gandhi, and others. In order to "Think Different," you have to be able to perceive differently. Since we all know that perception is in the eye of the beholder, shifting your perception gives you a different view of things and, thus, different ways of reacting.

On the road to success, solving problems is as important as thinking creatively. If we don't start with an accurate understanding of a problem or if we make a faulty analysis, our solutions will be wrong. Consider the following when you examine a situation to be sure that you perceive the problem correctly and that your solution is on track:

- Get deeply into the situation or problem. As Ogden Nash said, "*Confidence is the feeling you have before you really understand the problem.*" You can't understand a problem unless you study it, research it, and get involved in a way that brings you firsthand knowledge.

- Rearrange the elements of the problem. Usually there is a basic set of conditions that are part of the problem. Shifting them, seeking other positions, and moving them about will give you different views of the problem and suggest different solutions.

- Effectively use the information available. Too much information can get in the way of seeing a problem and how you choose to use the information. Decide what information is important and what is irrelevant. Carefully evaluate all the information available to decide what to discard and what weight to give to the information you decide to consider.

- Set aside your preconceived notions. It's not always easy to look at a problem objectively. Set aside your prejudices, your emotions, and personal gain. Separate these things out of your analysis so that you know how much your decision is affected by these personal factors and objectivity.

- Deconstruct the problem. Then put it back together in a variety of ways. Examine each of the new constructs to see if the best solution jumps out at you.

- Be aware of how your cultural biases affect your judgment. The culture we grow up in and work in does prejudice our decisions. Be sure that what you conclude is not inappropriately a product of your cultural bias.

- Know what your motivations are in relation to each solution that surfaces. Is there a selfish reason you lean to one solution over another? Is that good or bad? Is it what you want?

- How will you benefit from the decision? If you know beforehand how you will benefit, you can be objective in your analysis and can then decide whether to be partial to what will favorably affect you.

- What are the risks involved? As you develop a variety of solutions, think about the risk/reward ratio for each possibility. Is the reward you derive from the solution worth any risks that are inherent within the solution?

Decision making is nothing more than choosing between alternatives. When you look at a problem, analyze all the alternatives and come up with answers that serve you best. On your way to success, there will be a million small decisions that seem almost unimportant and a few very big ones that you know will change the course of your life. I don't advocate major analysis of all the small decisions, but I certainly do advocate it for the major ones. The small decisions, however, should not be left to the dictates of whim. They, too, need attention.

WE CAN ALL USE SOME HELP

Who among us can't use some help? If you say you don't need any, you're fooling yourself. Perhaps it is "machismo" that you've developed. Even women can develop this negative independence. Sometimes we feel we can do it all with no help from anyone. You can't! We all need a hand now and then.

I don't know of any successful person who has not been helped in some way along his or her path to success. Sometimes the help is unsolicited but, more often, it is sought. We get help from other people and help is out there for the picking. There is help at libraries, on the Internet, in schools, at government offices; there are almost endless sources of information on almost any topic in the world. You might say there is personal help and help from secondary sources.

We need help to see and to do. Other people's views often change our perception (as my wife changed my view of the painting) and can help us shift paradigms. Sharing ideas can clarify how we see and offer solutions. Besides needing people's opinions, we need relationships. Relationships enable us to draw upon their contacts, knowledge, support, and experience.

IDEAS AND INFORMATION FROM OBVIOUS AND ODD PLACES

Thomas Watson, who founded IBM in 1924, placed on the wall above and behind his desk a single framed word: THINK. It became the corporate motto of one of the most influential companies of this century.

THINK. The handiest source of new ideas is your own mind—your thoughts, wants, needs, and desires. Ideas may also come from the world around you.

Peter Drucker, the man who invented modern management, observed that most success comes from systematic innovations that exploit change. In his book *Innovation and Entrepreneurship* (Harper & Row, 1985), he defined seven specific kinds of change that are sources of innovation opportunity for business. I believe they are equally valid for individuals looking for help in seeing new opportunities and developing new ideas. Drucker suggests you look at the following:

1. The unexpected, including unexpected success, unexpected failure, unexpected events.

2. Incongruity between reality as it actually is and reality as it is assumed to be.

3. Innovation based on process need.

4. Changes in industry structure and market structure, especially those that catch everyone unaware.

5. Demographic shifts and population changes.

6. Changes in perception, mood, and meaning.

7. New knowledge, including the scientific and the nonscientific.

Open a book, open your mind, open a magazine, newspaper, business periodical, whatever. The key word is *Open*. Don't limit yourself to the publications in your field. I have found some of my best ideas and solutions to problems in books of fiction, philosophy, psychology, science, and yes, science fiction.

Write out a list of what you determine to be your required reading. Place publications in your field at the top of the list. When I was fully active in business, I constantly scanned and did selective reading in over sixty trade and business publications a month. In addition, I also read on average three books a week (a book on business, a non-fiction book, and a book of fiction). My business has always been dependent on ideas and the latest information. If your list is too long, narrow it down to the publications most likely to spark ideas. Don't put off this task. To augment the required reading that you customized for your special field, choose general publications you feel are essential for taking the pulse of change from the following list:

NEWSPAPERS

New York Times
Wall Street Journal
Your local newspaper

PERIODICALS

Business Week
Forbes
Fortune
News & World Report
Harvard Business Review (A monthly publication and my personal favorite, P.O. Box 52621, Boulder, CO 80321-2621)

STANDARD MONTHLY AND QUARTERLY REFERENCES

Economic Outlook, USA (published by Survey Research Center, University of Michigan, P.O. Box 1248, Ann Arbor, MI 48106)

Economic Indicators (Council of Economic Advisors) *Survey of Current Business* (U.S. Department of Commerce, Washington, DC 20230)

Business Conditions Digest (U.S. Department of Commerce, Washington, DC 20230)

Monthly Labor Review (U.S. Department of Labor, Washington, DC 20212)

Note: The four publications above are available from the U.S. Government Printing Office, Washington, DC 20402.

International Financial Statistics (IMF, Washington, DC, OECD Observer and Economic Outlook (700 19th Street NW, Washington, DC 20431)

STANDARD ANNUAL REFERENCES

Statistical Abstract (U.S. Department of Commerce) Economic Report of the President

Our Government Budget

Note: All of these are available from the U.S. Government Printing Office, Washington, DC 20402.

INTERNET

U.S. Department of Commerce
http://www.doc.gov

U.S. Department of Labor
http://stats.bls.gov

International Monetary Fund
http://www.inf.org

Libraries and universities are a great source of information. You can connect with them all over the world on the Internet, an endless source of information and ideas, particularly the World Wide Web (WWW). You can use one of the many search engine software tools available, such as Excite, Yahoo, AltaVista, WebCrawler, Looksmart, InfoSeek, and many others that help you locate a subject, company, or individual. Although I use the Internet a great deal, I still enjoy searching through books in our own library that we have accumulated over the years or browsing in public or university libraries.

For the few of you who may not know, the Internet is the name for a group of worldwide information resources linked together in an electronic network of electronic networks and accessible by anyone with a computer and a modem. A home page is an Internet site created by an individual or organization that contains hypertext links to data relevant to an individual or organization. A home page is like an electronic table of contents providing orderly access to whatever the individual or organization has to offer.

My Web Page Address is:
http://edbobrow.mcni.com/

Put Your Money on Yourself— Not on Your Helpers

Advice and help from others is valuable, but I wouldn't bet on them. I bet on myself and always have. In an earlier chapter, I related how not being fully involved with some companies my brother and I had acquired ended in failure. Here is a story of what can happen when you are fully involved.

For many years my parents owned two loft buildings on Broadway. They were losing money. When my folks moved to Florida, my Dad thought they should turn the buildings over to a real estate manager. He felt he was getting too old to bother with them. My Mom, who had always kept the books, was suffering from the beginning stages of Alzheimer's disease and could no longer handle that task. My Dad was convinced that we should find some way to make the buildings profitable, as he always felt they should remain in the family. Some advisors suggested we sell the buildings, take a profit, and reinvest in government securities so that the capital would return a sure income to my parents, an income they needed for their retirement.

Since my brother and I would inherit the buildings, Dad talked it over with us and said he was willing to turn them over if I took on the total responsibility of managing them and made sure that their retirement income was protected. Since I was intimately familiar with the buildings, I knew what I was dealing with. After careful analysis, I was able to figure out why we were losing money and decided to take on the management responsibility. I would use our sales agency's offices to handle the paperwork and bookkeeping. In my analysis I found that the losses were not in the operation of the buildings, but because my Dad had not paid attention to renting to quality tenants.

We consulted an architect about upgrading the buildings. He came up with plans and designs to convert the buildings to house antique companies and design firms. As I was responsible for the buildings' operation and responsible for a certain income for our parents, I decided that I didn't want to mortgage the future and risk a conversion. Instead, I decided to go after antique companies who would be willing to fix up their space to suit their needs. This kept our investment to a minimum. We were able to get two tenants in the antique business and the buildings began producing a small profit. We also avoided a major investment and began to turn a profit. We invested in some enhancements, such as painting, new boilers, repairs, and refurbishing. These renovations and the two anchor tenants attracted more tenants willing to pay higher rents.

Since the two buildings were operating smoothly and producing a profit, we thought it would be great if we could buy another building and had our eye on a building for sale. My brother and I looked it over and thought it could be turned into a moneymaking property. I consulted with my advisors, as I always did. They told us that the price was too high for what we wanted to do. We argued with them but, at that time, we were not as experienced as they were, so we bowed to their analysis. It was a mistake. What we thought would happen on that block did happen—the property went up in value. Someone else bought the building and converted it, and, from what we understand, profited from it. We have always been sorry that we didn't bet on ourselves and that we let ourselves be talked out of what we believed in.

THEY DON'T HAVE TO LIVE THEIR ADVICE—YOU DO

There is more to the story about the two buildings on Broadway. Because I had turned the buildings around, they became desirable property. While I was away on one of my business trips, my wife received a call from a real estate broker asking if we wanted to sell the buildings. We had often discussed never selling the buildings and that we would rather try to acquire an additional building. She told him we absolutely did not want to sell but were interested in buying a building. Instead of hanging up after saying no, she asked if the buildings on either side of ours were for sale. The broker, who had not thought to suggest it, did have a building for sale adjacent to ours. My wife also told him she was sure I would be interested and that I would meet with him as soon as I returned. We met and, although the price in my view was about 10 percent higher than market, I made a verbal commitment on the spot. I just had to call him back with the details necessary to draw up the contract. I had been in touch with my brother by phone and knew he agreed it was a good deal for us. Before signing the contract for the purchase, we reviewed the facts. We both agreed that owning 75 feet of frontage on Broadway instead of the 50 feet we had would increase the resale value of the three buildings, probably threefold. We also felt we could upgrade the tenants, as we had done with our other buildings. We made the deal. Betting on ourselves worked out extremely well.

Summary: We consulted with people who could help us; we got ideas from them; we broke the paradigm of what the buildings could be; we analyzed carefully; then we bet on our own ability to produce the income we wanted. Years later, when we sold the three buildings, we made a handsome profit, one much greater than if we had only owned two of them. The help from others was valuable, but the decision and responsibility was ours. If it hadn't worked out, it would have been our mistake. If we had followed the advice of some of the people we consulted, it would have been their mistake and we would have had to live with it.

10

NO ONE LIVES YOUR LIFE BUT YOU

We are all in this—alone.

—Reported to have been said by Lily Tomlin

Y ou might think it's cynical to say, "We are all in this—alone." But when you're in pain, no one feels it but you. Others may sympathize and those dear and near will hurt for you, but you and you alone carry the burden of your pain. Often friends say to me, "My back went out. It really hurts." Then they remember my back problems and quickly add, "But nothing like the way your back hurts you." My answer is always, "Whatever pain you have, it's your pain. It's what you feel. It cannot and should not be compared to anyone else's. Your hurt is the worst because it is *yours*. It is what you, and you alone, feel." In the same way, you and you alone make decisions for yourself. No one else lives your life but you. Your decisions and their successes and failures are yours. You own them, you are responsible for them, and you have to live with them.

A friend of mine once told me about a particular company listed on the NASDAQ stock exchange. He was the third largest investor in the company and very positive about its growth potential or he would not have invested as heavily as he did. He suggested that I invest in the company, too. He personally had nothing to gain from my buying the stock as it was selling very well over the exchange. He just wanted me to make some money from what he believed in.

Even though he invested heavily and, in his expert judgment, the stock was sure to go up, he cautioned that nothing was guaranteed. I told him that I was a "big boy" and would make the decision based on my own analysis, not just on his recommendation. If things didn't work out as he expected, it would be my responsibility, not his. I would live with my decision. When I bought the stock I didn't invest more than I could afford to lose. Though it never worked out to be the winner my friend thought it would be, I took my losses and never held him responsible. Since I had weighed the pros and cons of investing after considering his recommendation, I could never blame him for what I chose to do. It was my life I was dealing with, and no one lives my life but me.

THE ABCS OF LIFE

Just as your pain is yours alone, you alone are the final arbiter of your actions in your quest for success. Success is your personal challenge and responsibility. I came across a guide that might prove helpful in living the life that only you can live. I received it via the Internet. It is called the ABCs. The original thoughts are in boldface type, with my comments in normal type.

A-void negative sources, people, things, and habits. Developing a positive attitude and associating with "can do" people will help you attain success. One of my friends, a very successful "can do" attorney, says, "One's frame of mind plays a major role in one's success." In and of itself, however, it will not bring you success. There is more involved than a positive attitude. But avoiding the negative and accentuating the positive will be a big help toward reaching your goals. You might want read an old book, *The Power of Positive Thinking* by Dr. Norman Vincent Peale (Ballantine, 1996). Dr. Peale advocated changing your life by developing a positive attitude. While the book is inspirational and has helped many people, it holds no magic formula.

B-elieve in yourself. What helps most to gain a belief in yourself is to achieve small victories and then build on them. If you don't have a strong belief in yourself now, set some small goals. As you achieve these small goals, set some that are a little bigger. As those succeed, set even bigger ones. You will find that as each goal is achieved, it will give you a little more confidence to achieve the next goal.

C-onsider things from every angle. In the last chapter, I suggested doing research, obtaining advice, and deconstructing situations or problems to see them from every angle. It is often hard to be objective, particularly when you want things rather badly. If, however, you examine your options from all angles, you are less likely to make mistakes.

D-on't give up and don't give in. Persistence and insistence are essential to success. If you give up at the first challenge, failure, or disappointment, you are not likely to achieve success. Believe in your dreams and in your goals. Pursue them relentlessly and only give up if reality shows that these goals were not realistically chosen.

E-njoy life today. Yesterday is gone and tomorrow may never come. To live in the present is one of the most difficult things to do. We spend more time thinking about the past and dreaming of the future than we spend in the present moment. Not that there isn't value in examining history and dreaming of the future—there is. But you cheat yourself when you can't be fully focused on what you are doing now. Not only do you lose the possible pleasure of the moment, you lose the ability to direct your present actions to achieve your future hopes and dreams.

F-amily and friends are hidden treasures.
Seek them and enjoy their riches. Aristotle said that
the summa bona (greatest good) of life was intellectual activity. Certainly intellectual activity is one of
the very great goods in life. But without people to be
close to, to love and be loved, we do not have the
emotional base for intellectual activity. We need the
comfort, support, and love of family and friends in
order to pursue whatever is necessary to become a
success. We also need the help of our family and
friends in the pursuit of our life's goals to give counsel,
help make contacts, and open doors to the future for us.

G-ive more than you planned to give. There
are some people who want to get everything in life
for free. They do nothing and want everything. This
is contrary to the laws of nature: nothing comes from
nothing. These people do the bare minimum and
only when they absolutely must. There are others
who will only do what they have to, not a lick more.
Then there are the successful people who give full
measure and a bit extra. Full measure and a little extra
is a good philosophy and good business. I'm sure you
like to deal with people who give their all and then
a little extra. I have found that being fully involved in
what I'm doing and giving that little extra usually
brings me greater satisfaction, enjoyment, and even
money. In my business, it also makes for satisfied and
repeat clients. The extra value in all you do makes you
feel good and you become more valuable to others.

H-ang onto your dreams. Throughout the book I have been coaching you not only to hold onto your dreams, but also to turn them into reality through planning and persistence. You might have to change your strategies when things are not going your way, but persist in your goals so that you can achieve your dreams. Don't give them up easily.

I-gnore those who try to discourage you. You will run across many naysayers in your life, people who pooh-pooh everything: "This won't work" or "That's not a good idea." In general, they never have an encouraging word. You must distinguish between these people and people who give you genuinely good advice—people who counsel you well, who may sometimes discourage you from taking a particular path, but who are just as likely to encourage you.

J-ust do it! Planning is great, up to a point. There are some people who seem to always be planning but never doing. There is a time when "just do it" is good advice. In the chapter, "Let's Get Down to Action," I discuss in detail when it is important to go directly to action, when to plan, and when to stop planning and begin to act.

K-eep on trying, no matter how hard it seems. It will get better. I had a very wise grandmother who always used to tell me to hang in there when things got very rough, that "this, too, will change." The one thing any of us can be sure of is that, no matter what, good or bad, the situation will change.

L–ove yourself first and foremost. If you don't know who you are or what you're about in this life, it will be hard for you to love yourself. If you accept yourself, respect yourself, have confidence in yourself, and love yourself for who and what you are, it is easier to love others. Everything starts with the self, for it is through yourself that you see and react to the world.

M–ake it happen. What happens in your life and how you react to what you can't control is primarily up to you. Make the best of things you can't control. There is a lot you can make happen if you know what you want, have a plan for getting it, and work hard to obtain it. To make it happen isn't easy. It takes a lot of effort and hard work, but the reward and satisfaction of having "made it happen" is extremely fulfilling.

N–ever lie, cheat, or steal. Always strike a fair deal. This sounds like "Mama says" and "saluting the flag." It may be, but it's also a good practice that brings its own rewards. Honesty makes people want to trust you and deal with you. Fairness brings people back into relationships with you over and over again. Think how you feel about people who lie and cheat and how you feel about people who give you an honest shake. Honesty should be axiomatic and important to keep in mind when that devil "greed" rears its head, when it wants you to lie just a little or cheat so that you can win a few extra dollars. If you listen to that little devil, you may win those extra dollars, but you are sure to lose more if others turn away from you as a result.

O-pen your eyes and see things as they really are. We spent almost a whole chapter on really seeing and on paradigms in an effort to get you to see in different ways, to break old habits of seeing. This is a reminder: Don't just look—see as deeply as possible. Whatever you're looking at—the sunset, a tree, your child, a problem, an opportunity, whatever— seeing, not just looking, will give you deep satisfaction and will often bring new understanding that leads to success.

P-ractice makes perfect. In my experience, people who are the most successful have prepared themselves for whatever they undertake in life. No one becomes famous or successful without preparation. My closest friend, next to my wife, is a very successful criminal attorney. He has been practicing for many, many years. Yet whenever he goes to trial, he prepares and prepares and prepares. He has always said, "Preparation is the key to victory."

Q-uitters never win and winners never quit. Although there are times when you need to cut your losses, I don't consider that quitting. I consider it re- grouping. Quitting is when you give up on your goal. Cutting your losses occurs when you regroup your resources, both personal and monetary, in order to try again, perhaps in a different way. You may have to change strategies, but you should not have to change your goal.

R-ead, study, and learn about everything important in your life. Some of us are "learning people" who spend our lives studying and learning, curious and interested to acquire more and more knowledge. People like this can take advantage of and fit into our present information age. They are interesting, vital, and successful people who are vibrant and alive. If they happen to be action-oriented as well, they often become the great accomplishers. You, too, can fly high on the wings of knowledge if you integrate and apply what you learn.

S-top procrastinating. We all tend to put off doing for one reason or another. If you're a procrastinator, you probably don't realize how much of life you're missing. Life is in the doing. When things are put off to watch another TV show or engage in some other passive activity, you miss the opportunity to be engaged, active, and productive. When you have tasks that are distasteful, routine, and boring, it helps if you relegate them to habit. Get them done and out of the way so that you can get to more interesting things in life with a clear mind.

T-ake control of your own destiny. This is really what this chapter and the entire book is all about. Living your own life can only be done if you are in control of your life.

U-understand yourself in order to better understand others. To understand is a great power. If you understand yourself, you can use your talents better and achieve your goals more easily. The better you understand yourself, the more you will understand others.

V-visualize it. May you always have a vision, a dream to reach out for and achieve! If you also develop foresight—the ability to see the future as a result of your actions—it will prove to be a great precursor to success.

W-ant it more than anything. Have passion for what you believe in and what you do. Believe in it; believe in yourself; feel it deeply. People know when you feel passionately and are passionately behind what you say and do. This level of enthusiasm helps rally people to your cause.

X-celebrate your efforts. When you don't procrastinate, it speeds up your efforts; but don't run so fast that you stumble!

Y-ou are unique of all Nature's creations. Nothing can replace you. Believe it!

Z-ero in on your target, and go for it! Be a success!

Some of the ABCs may sound a bit corny; that doesn't make them any less true or useful. If you don't dismiss them as old saws but think about them and embrace them, you will find their wisdom and inspiration will serve you well on your path to success.

EXAMINE YOUR POTENTIAL REALISTICALLY

> *"The life which is unexamined*
> *is not worth living.*
>
> —Plato, *Dialogues,* "Phaedrus," sec.38

To live your own life, you need a firm grasp of your potential. Sometimes it's not possible because you haven't had the opportunity to test yourself or haven't had an occasion to use your knowledge or experience. It is the realistic assessment of what you do know, what you don't know, and what you need to learn that is necessary to realize your goals and become successful.

Before you can examine your potential, know what is required to achieve a particular goal. If you want to become an architect, for example, know in as much detail as possible the aptitudes that are required and what the necessary skill sets are in order to be successful in that field. Ask yourself these questions:

1. **Aptitudes:** Do I need good spatial perception, skill in mathematics, engineering abilities, ability to sketch, or any other specific skills?

2. **Knowledge:** Do I know the requirements of the formal education I need to meet licensing requirements? How much schooling is needed, what kind of schooling, which schools are best?

3. **Practical Skills:** Most important—do I know the practical, everyday demands of the profession? Will I be drawing plans, meeting with people, managing others, selling my services?

There are aptitude and psychological tests you can take and use as a guide in determining your basic aptitudes and psychological inclination for almost any type of work. You can also visit architectural firms and talk with people in the profession to hear their views about their work. Study journals, trade publications, and books on the subject.

Whichever field you choose to enter, whatever work you do, it is necessary to understand what is required so that you can measure your current knowledge, skills, and abilities against what is needed. Work on filling the gap between the knowledge you possess and what you need to acquire. In general, study everything you will need to achieve your goal of matching your likes and dislikes, skills and aptitudes, and desires with the reality of the work.

The best way to obtain skills is to practice. The best way to gain knowledge is to study. The best way to integrate your skills and knowledge is to apply them.

HABITS: GOOD, BAD, AND INDIFFERENT

A big question: Are the habits we have the ones we want and need? Too often we operate on automatic and take for granted that the only means we have to respond in any situation is through established habits. We fail to examine our habits; we arbitrarily decide to change this one, establish a new one, or hold to an old one. You and you alone lead the life you live. Habits play an important role in how we live our lives. I hope you will seriously examine your habits, particularly in the light of the habits described in this chapter. These habits are the ones that most successful people seem to have, habits that I believe you need to acquire in order to be successful.

Before talking about the habits of the successful, let me tell you how I changed a major bad habit. Perhaps my method will be of help to you. I discovered this technique years ago when I was about fifteen to twenty pounds overweight. I had just seen my doctor about the relentless pains in my back and joints. He told me that if I could lose weight it would more than likely take pressure off my joints and ease my pain. Since I was just beginning a regimen of physical therapy, we both thought this was a good time for me to also lose weight. He pointed out that the overhang of my stomach and lack of muscle strength in that area contributed to my pain. Pain is a powerful motivator and I was motivated!

I knew it would be difficult to give up all the things I liked to eat and drink. I didn't believe in diet programs, but I did believe in myself and my own ability to take charge of my destiny. If losing weight and getting back into physical shape would help, I was going to do it. I decided to cut down on my food intake at mealtimes and on my nibbling during the day and evenings. The best diet for me was to cut out all eating between meals and to reduce my portions at mealtimes. This way I could still eat almost everything I liked, but in smaller portions. I started by leaving one third of the food on my plate; later I left 25 percent of what was served to me. I also stopped drinking anything except water between meals. I restricted myself to one scotch a day and, on special occasions, added a glass of wine. This diet, coupled with exercise, worked. I lost fifteen pounds. It was difficult at first—it always is when you change a habit.

How was I able to break old eating habits and establish new ones? I set goals by the day, by the week, and by the month. I was disciplined. I asked my family and friends to support my effort; I committed myself by going public with what I expected to achieve. I also used a small but effective device: I wrote notes to myself. I stuck the notes in the cookie jar, on the refrigerator, in my jacket pockets, on my money clip, in my desk drawer, and just about anywhere else I might think of food or reach out for a treat. I wrote funny sayings, strict admonishments, and inspirational messages on the notes. Believe it or not, those notes were effective reminders of what I planned to do. They reinforced my efforts.

That was about fifteen years ago. I reached my goal—a weight that fluctuated between 175 to 180 pounds. As a result, I had less pain, no stomach overhang, and generally felt better. As a matter of fact, within the past two years I switched to a low carbohydrate and high protein diet. Again, I used the note-writing technique. Now my weight fluctuates between 170 and 175. I feel I am now at my optimal weight. Naturally, I had trouble adjusting my diet both times. Who said getting what you want in life is easy! It was, however, worth the effort. I know you can achieve the same results in whatever you attempt, if you truly want to.

TWENTY-THREE HABITS FOR SUCCESS

Here is a list of twenty-three habits I believe a person needs to develop to be truly successful:

1. **Ambition.** You have to really want it; be willing to go after it, whatever it is. Ambition is not the province of those who only

want to make a lot of money. You can be
ambitious for your own personal success
and for whatever you undertake.

2. **Analyze.** Research, assembling facts, analysis, and thinking things through are
   essential to the choices you make.

3. **Budget your energy and time.** Your
   energy and time are your most precious
   resources. Direct and allocate them wisely
   and carefully.

4. **Commitment.** It inspires others and yourself when you are committed to a cause and
   stand by your commitment. Commitment
   should also extend to your values, ambitions,
   goals, integrity, and standards.

5. **Discipline.** You must have the resolve to
   discipline yourself to do whatever is
   required to achieve your goals. That doesn't
   mean doing it when you can get to it, like
   tomorrow or when the spirit moves you.

6. **Enthusiasm.** Show you believe in what
   you set out to do. People need to catch
   your enthusiasm and know that you are a
   believer down to your toes.

7. **Faith in yourself.** Unless you believe in
   yourself you can't expect others to believe
   in you. The great successes in this world are

people who believed strongly in themselves even when the rest of the world did not.

8. **Flexibility.** Know when you have to be flexible. I always think of the strength of bamboo grass. It bends with the wind, but it keeps growing. There will be times when progress is best made by being flexible.

9. **Going the extra mile.** It adds momentum to your efforts and gives added value to all that you do.

10. **Initiative.** In order to lead and to achieve, you have to act. As one old general said, "Be the firstest with the mostest." Take the initiative; it's the way to win victories.

11. **Inspiring others.** Whatever you do in life you will need the support of others—their confidence, their belief in you, but their backing often needs to be inspired.

12. **Intuitiveness.** Listen to and trust your inner self. Never make a final decision on any matter until your analysis and your gut feeling are in agreement. If it doesn't feel right after carefully processing the information, it probably is not right for you.

13. **Know yourself.** To know yourself is an ongoing process. You are constantly changing as you grow and move through

life. That's why you must make it a habit to reexamine yourself regularly to see if you're still the person you thought you were and if the goals you have set are still appropriate.

14. **Learn from failure.** Always analyze why something failed and how you could have turned it into a success. We all learn more from our failures than from our successes.

15. **Motivate yourself.** Self-motivation is an essential part of being able to move yourself from wanting to doing. No one can really motivate you. They can sometimes offer something that triggers your motivational drive, but only you can motivate yourself.

16. **No fear of failure.** The road to success is built on failures.

17. **Positive attitude.** There is nothing that builds confidence more, in yourself and in others, than a positive attitude. Be sure of your position, however, because if you're wrong, your future positive attitude may not carry the credibility that you would like it to.

18. **Prioritize.** Know what is of primary importance in every situation.

19. **Purposefulness.** Without purpose, a vision, goals, and a plan, you won't be clear

which of life's roads you want to take. It's also important for others to know your purpose so they can help you toward your goals or follow you to your purposeful end.

20. **Set goals.** As I have said throughout this book, you must have goals and know what you want. Others will often be of help to you on the road to achieving them if you share your goals with them.

21. **Think WIN.** Always think that you can and will win.

22. **Vision.** Vision has two meanings here. It means to develop foresight and also to have a dream or vision to pursue and share with others.

23. **Work hard.** As Thomas Edison said, "Genius is one percent inspiration and ninety-nine percent perspiration." A cliché, but always true.

It may not always be easy to keep all twenty-three of these characteristics in mind. It may even be more difficult to turn them into habits. But if you do, you will have gone a long way toward turning yourself into a successful person.

Part IV

The Tools of Success

Achieve the success you plan for by using everything at your disposal.

11

The Best Tools Are Tailor-Made

It is possible to fail in many ways ... while to succeed is possible only in one way (for which reason also one is easy and the other difficult— to miss the mark easy, to hit it difficult).

—Aristotle, *Nicomacean Ethics,* Book 1, Ch.6

I never said it would be easy—I did say it can be done! Each and every one of you can be a success if you really want to, if you apply yourself. Only a few of you will become millionaires, stars, or famous. But you can all be winners at life and successful many times over by meeting your personal success goals.

For every job there are special tools: Carpenters and plumbers have their tools, physicians have another set of tools, and lawyers yet another. It is the same with success.

You need the right set of tools for the particular success you are seeking. If you want to be successful financially, you need a different set of tools than if you set out to achieve success as a writer.

Has this happened to you? You intended to make a lot of money but, when you set out to do it, you found yourself floundering. You didn't know where to begin and whatever you tried did not work. There was a period in my life when that happened to me. I had virtually no money but wanted to make a lot by clinching a "big deal," which was to buy and run a good-size company. I thought that Dr. Posner Shoes, my former employer, was a good target. Herbert Posner, the president, was getting on in years and there was no one in the company he felt could succeed him. I was young enough and egotistical enough to think that I could.

The problem was that I had not yet networked sufficiently to have contacts who could help me raise cash. I had no prior experience in running a company and was totally unfamiliar with acquisitions. Nevertheless, I visited my local bank to get some advice. The bank referred me to someone who was a "deal maker." He wasn't interested in my plan but was kind enough to offer me advice. He advised me to go to the big banking houses and walk in as if I owned the place. He recommended that I act very self-assured and show extreme confidence in what I presented. He also told me that I should know the

financials backward and forward, know what I
wanted, and project an aura of past successes. Well,
I didn't know the financials. I had no past success and
couldn't act as though I did. I was able to project
some self-confidence, but the source of it was my
drive and ambition. I knew I could get analytical
support on the financials from my accountant, if I
could obtain statements from Posner. I had already
spoken with Herbert Posner about my idea to acquire his company. If I could demonstrate the ability
to raise the money, he was willing to share his financials
with me. But the finance people wanted statements
before they would consider investing any money. A
true chicken and egg situation.

The more I researched and networked, I realized
I was not the kind of person who could pull off a deal
like that. I just did not have the knowledge and financial backing. I did learn, though, that it was great
to have a big dream, even though I didn't have the
panache to pull it off. My failure taught me that before getting involved in trying to get what I wanted,
I needed the required tools to do the job. If I had first
acquired the tools I needed—an understanding of the
financials, contacts to raise money, and previous successful operation of a company—I might have been
successful. Wanting it and believing I could do it,
without knowing what was involved in order to get
it, could produce no other outcome but failure. A
valuable lesson!

SEVEN STEPS TO DETERMINE THE TOOLS YOU WILL NEED

To know your dream is not enough. You must be able to convert that dream into concrete goals. Only then can you begin to figure out what tools you will need to fulfill your dream. Here is a process to help you to determine these tools:

1. Research what the situation requires in order to turn your dream into reality.

2. List all the skills, competencies, and information needed to succeed in a particular situation.

3. Check your list with at least three people who are experienced in the same or a similar situation. They will confirm, deny, and perhaps add to your list.

4. From your list, check off the skills, competencies, and information you believe you already have.

5. Make a list of the skills, competencies, and information that you still need. Add any others recommended to you or that come to mind. This will be a list of the tools you must acquire.

6. Rate the items on the list: M = Must have, L = Like to have, and D = Don't really need.

7. Convert each item on your list that is an M or an L into a goal. Under each of the goals, list the strategies you will use to achieve it.

Following these seven steps will enable you to develop a program to go after the tools you need to accomplish the larger goal—achieving your dreams or vision.

After listing all the required tools, set up a worksheet similar to the one illustrated below.

	TOOLS NEEDED	RATING
1.	Learn to analyze financial statements.	M
2.	Obtain experience in running a company.	M
3.	Network in the financial community.	M
4.	Study cases of acquisitions.	L
5.	Get a Masters of Business Administration (MBA).	D

When you have completed your list of tools, set them up as your goals, and then develop strategies for them on a worksheet, as shown in the following table.

TOOLS NEEDED	STRATEGIES TO ACQUIRE THEM
1. Learn to analyze financial statements.	A. Take a seminar.
	B. Review and study with accountant.
	C. Get books to read.
2. Obtain experience in running a company.	A. Look for a position as CEO.
	B. Start a company.
	C. Read books on management.
	D. Read books on operations.
3. Network in the financial community.	A. Join the New York Venture Group.
	B. Attend breakfast meetings with New York Venture Group.

TOOLS NEEDED	STRATEGIES TO ACQUIRE THEM	
	C.	Start networking.
	D.	Start and maintain a database of contacts.
4. Study cases of acquisitions.	A.	Read Harvard Business Review.
	B.	Check Internet for cases to study.
	C.	Start an MBA program at NYU.

Note: New York Venture Group, care of New York Business Forums, Inc., 605 Madison Avenue, Suite 300, New York, NY 10022-1901; e-mail to **info@nybusinessforums.com**

GATHER AND ANALYZE INFORMATION

This section is based on information provided by Joanne F. Gucwa, Technology Management Associates, Inc., Chicago, Illinois. This company obtains information globally and helps clients to understand the information and then use it.

e-mail: jogucwa@techmange.com
Home page: http://www.techmanage.com

Research, information, and knowledge are the most important keys to success. If you don't research properly, gain accurate information, and turn the information you gather into usable knowledge, it is not likely that you will have a basis upon which to make an accurate analysis.

When you do research or gather information, don't trust a single source. It doesn't matter whether that source is an individual, a search engine on the Internet, a book, or another authority. You must gather from enough sources so that you are comfortable that what you learn is fact, opinion, or generally accepted information. Don't misunderstand—all types of information can be valuable, but when you're betting your future on what you learn, you want as many hard facts as you can find.

As an example, here is what Joanne Gucwa had to say about not going to just one source for information.

> It was reported in the *Wall Street Journal* that the search engine with the most coverage of the World Wide Web (WWW) only hit a third of the total estimated sites out there. The others, including the most popular, search far fewer, covering 20 percent or so of all sites.... We were asked to look at the

trends in titanium use in a couple of industries. This was at a time when several developing countries were planning on bringing new mines on stream, perhaps doubling the world's then-current output. Now, whether you are a producer or a user of titanium, you know what that means. Lower prices. Long-term purchasing contracts would be in jeopardy and would probably have to be re-negotiated, on the one hand; new applications that would have been too expensive in the past could now be feasible, on the other. If you were a producer, what would be the impact on shareholder value if prices would plummet? As a user, what would you do with your savings? Increase retained earnings or dividend payout? New directions in R&D? Critical questions, no? I hit my top five favorite search engines, and guess what? Got just about the same hits with each one of them. And I wasn't finding what I KNEW was out there. A friend out in California suggested a hot new search engine I hadn't even heard of. Tried it and... BINGO! Everything from NASA and DOD sites (all non-classified!) to trade associations, to white papers."

ELEVEN KEYS TO GATHERING INFORMATION

Here is what you can do to effectively gather information:

1. Prepare a list of the things you want to find out.

2. Make a list of the questions you will ask and seek to have answered by the people you talk with and/or through your research.

3. If you are having trouble finding what you want, ask. Ask everyone you come in contact with if they can suggest where you might find the information. This includes contacts you make in person, on the Internet, or through any other means. When I was researching a project, many times one contact led to another that led to another, and finally to the source for the information I needed.

4. Just as you should not trust a single source, do not trust a single medium. Besides the Internet, try such media as association executives, editors of trade journals, consultants, not-for-profit organizations, and people in the organizational trenches.

5. Do some reading and homework before calling anyone for information. When you already have some basic background, you hit the ground running and won't waste the time of the people you contact. You will also get a much higher level of information if you start a telephone conversation by saying, "I discovered such-and-such in my research and I wanted to get a more in-depth perspective from you."

6. Don't use one name, key word, or phrase to describe what you're trying to find on the Internet. For example, a car is also an auto, a vehicle, and transportation. Use phrases that incorporate the various descriptors that would be used.

7. Build your own library of information. I have information gathered from various sources that I store in print (primarily books) or electronically to help in my personal planning. I also become a valuable source of information for clients, colleagues, and others with whom I network. I also find material from previous searches for my articles, books, and the classes I teach. A word of caution: Date your material. In today's world things change very quickly and a particular situation may call for the most current research.

8. When you are researching, make detailed notes. Record the contact date(s), source, individual(s) contacted, and your findings. You never know when you will need to re-contact a source for more detail or information.

9. Leave no stone unturned; be creative. Venture beyond the tried and true. Check out Websites of not-for-profit organizations and special interest groups.

10. If you are looking for a job, trying to sell something, or negotiating with someone, do some homework before you visit with him or her. Check out the company's Website. If their stock is publicly traded, get their annual report and/or their 10K SEC filing. You can often find this information on the company's Website, at a brokerage house, or by calling the company and asking.

11. The amount of data and information you will need changes according to circumstances and strategic style. Timing is often critical, and not only in the world of high tech. Leverage the technological and personal resources available to whatever extent you can in order to get the information you need in the time frame you need it.

ANALYZE INFORMATION

To analyze is to go from information to understanding. There are numerous ways to take data apart, some useful, some not. Information by itself isn't worth very much. It's what you do with it that counts. The objective of most research is to uncover ways to improve a situation. Your analysis should focus on what your research implies, or what you might call the "so what?" factor. When you get information, say to yourself, "Now I know this—so what?" That "so what?" can drive the kinds and depth of analytical hoops through which you want to make the data jump in order to find relevant information, derive valid conclusions, and understand the information that will enable you to make good decisions.

Here are some guidelines that will shed light on the meaning behind the data you collect:

1. Don't characterize an elephant from its trunk alone and thus place undue reliance on far too few observations.

2. Data collection and analysis should be ongoing according to your needs. Therefore, set up a process to constantly monitor what will impact your goals.

3. Slice and dice the information. Relate the unrelated to find relationships that are not readily obvious. This process will help keep

you out of confining boxes and help break paradigms.

4. Depend more on what people do, less on what they say. This means to get their opinions, but watch their actions. Perception may be reality to the perceiver, but not necessarily reality to the researcher. For example, if you ask people how many seconds they've waited for an elevator or stood in the checkout line, more than 90 percent of the time their inner clock senses a lot more elapsed time than what their watch actually shows. If you ask them whether the ride or line was short or long, you would receive an answer based on this perception. If, however, you observed them and clocked the elevator ride or time spent in line, you would know the actual time spent.

5. Don't forget to take into account inevitability, universal truths, and common sense.

6. When all the data is in, ask yourself if there are new opportunities that you're missing.

7. Now, what does all this mean to you, your goals, and your plans?

Curiosity didn't kill the cat.
Complacency did.

—Joanne F. Gucwa, Technology Management Associates, Inc.

NETWORKING: THE UNIVERSAL TOOL

Networking is one of the most valuable tools you can employ when building toward success. For the sake of clarity, here are the dictionary definitions of "network" and "networking" according to Webster's *Ninth New Collegiate Dictionary:* Network is defined as "an interconnected or interrelated chain, group, or system" and networking is defined as "the exchange of information or services among individuals, groups, or institutions." For our purposes, networking is a system used to develop personal contacts that help us achieve success.

We all network, intentionally or unintentionally. It starts with family and friends when we are children. At school, we add some of the people we meet there to our network. As life moves on, some people who were part of our early years network are dropped; some are maintained, often for life. An unintentional network develops just from living. What I advocate is the deliberate establishment of a network of people with whom you have shared interests and values—people you feel you can help and who can help you.

It's a good idea to network on an ongoing basis, even when you're not sure of your goals. The most effective network has purpose behind it and is goal-driven. You might find yourself with these particular network needs:

- To find a job

- To sell something
- When you have a need to create something
- To attract support for yourself or for a cause
- When you need advice
- To develop suppliers
- To find the right someone who can help you
- Virtually anything for which you may need the assistance of others

Networking is interconnecting with others so that you and they can multiply knowledge, contacts, and resources.

WHY NETWORK?

My old friend, Ken Erdman, in a book he co-authored with Tom Sullivan, *Network Your Way to Success* (Marketers Bookshelf, 1992; 402 Bethlehem Pike, Philadelphia, PA, 19118), summed up all the various definitions of networking as "disciplined acquaintanceship." Exercise disciplined acquaintanceship always. When you have set your goals, it is even more important that you direct your efforts toward the kind of acquaintanceship that can help you succeed.

I first met Ken at the first national meeting of the Manufacturers Agents National Association (MANA) where I gave the keynote address. Ken came up to me and introduced himself. We talked for a while and found we had a great deal in common. We were both manufacturers' agents, had collateral businesses, and wrote and spoke nationally. We exchanged business cards and periodically kept in touch. We would phone one another if we had questions about how to handle certain situations.

Then we came up with the idea of giving a series of workshops for the people who managed independent sales agent's salesforces. I believe it was actually Ken's idea. I had just written a book, *Marketing Through Manufacturers' Agents,* one of the first to deal with the subject. With his contacts and mine, Ken thought we could draw enough people to make a workshop profitable and worth the effort. We held several of these workshops—none made money, but neither did we lose money. The benefit we each garnered from these workshops was well worth the effort. We expanded our contacts, learned by teaching, and obtained additional business from the exposure. If that had been the only thing we ever did together, it would have been a worthwhile result of networking. Ken and I keep in touch to this day. He has sold his agency business, as I have, and is involved in other business activities. Whenever either of us has a question or needs a contact the other might have, we phone each other. We have supported and helped each other over the years and have met other people and added them to our networks because of our connection.

NETWORKING IS
A TWO-WAY STREET

Networking is a systematized approach to making
and keeping your contacts. Reach out to them when
you need help, but also reach out to your contacts in
order to help them. When I started to network, we
used business cards as our network list. I converted
all my contacts into mailing and phone lists. At one
point we had a mailing list of over 5,000 names for
our promotional pieces and for our newsletter, the
"Bobrow Report." Today I still publish the report—
irregularly, not bimonthly as in the past. My newsletter maintains my network and lets people know
I'm still alive and actively consulting. Until recently
the format for our newsletter was four to six pages,
folded to fit a number ten envelope. Now I keep in
touch by e-mail and am considering publishing an
electronic newsletter. One bit of advice: If you
decide to publish a newsletter, make it "you oriented," not "me oriented."

Today my networking list of about 800 people is
kept in my computer. The names are sorted into
groups, such as consultants, family, friends, prospects,
utilities, school, students, Asia, Israel, and others. I
also have a program that reminds me when to call
certain people. In this way I keep in touch with some
people regularly by phone and others periodically by
e-mail, "snail mail," and fax. I can enter notes into

my database so that I know when special events are to occur. For example, I have been sending birthday and anniversary cards to certain people for years. I even phone some of them on their special day. In the past (pre-computers), I kept a special diary book for listing events. Once a month I wrote out all the cards I wanted to send, then put them in my daily follow-up file so I wouldn't forget to mail them at the appropriate time.

Now I keep these contacts for my own use and for others to use as well. At this stage in life, I am often of more help to others than they can be to me. I also keep my contacts because I care about the people. They interest me, are in the same field, or have similar interests. Perhaps I can help them and, of course, I might want to call upon them when and if I need help or a new contact.

ELEVEN GOOD NETWORKING SKILLS

If you apply the list below it will help you develop good networking skills:

1. **Be a good communicator.** Networking hinges on your ability to keep in touch. Otherwise, all you have is a list of people you once met.

2. **Be assertive.** You need to be able to ini-
   tiate contact even if you are shy. Sometimes
   it can be difficult. There are two key phrases
   that help break the ice: "Can you help me?"
   and "I have an idea for you."

3. **Be creative in your contacts**. It's bene-
   ficial to have creative ways to keep in touch
   or to make each new contact—ways to
   catch attention. Make a game of it.

4. **Be sincere.** Insincerity can usually be
   spotted. People don't want to help if you
   use false flattery or if they feel you always
   contact them for a selfish purpose.

5. **Be unselfish.** Go the extra mile. Give and
   give, whenever you can. It builds the relationship. Try to do things that will interest
   and help the other person.

6. **Be willing to share.** Don't play things
   close to the vest. If you don't share with
   others, it's not likely they will be willing to
   share with you.

7. **Know how to listen.** Just as there are times
   you need someone to listen to you, you
   must be willing to listen to others. There are
   two values to listening. It helps the other
   person and you may learn something.

8. **Be honest and non-manipulative.**
   Sooner or later dishonesty is discovered. If you intentionally mislead, you will soon be out of that person's network.

9. **Pass on information.** Be on the lookout for articles and other information to send to people in your network. People appreciate receiving information about things that interest them, just as you do.

10. **Start with an attitude that you want to help others and your efforts will come back tenfold.** If you sincerely want to help others, they will respond.

11. **Think of how you can help the other person.** Always keep your network's interests in mind. Look out for them and, more often than not, they will look out for you.

FOURTEEN PLACES FOR DEVELOPING A BASE OF CONTACTS

There are many places for developing a solid base of contacts—your family, your friends, and your social acquaintances. The best and most useful contacts usually come from business or professional areas. Here are some other ideas of where to find people to network with:

1. Workshops and seminars

2. Political meetings

3. Social events

4. Religious events

5. School

6. Vacations

7. Traveling

8. Business meetings

9. Clubs

10. Charitable organizations

11. Fraternal organizations

12. Sporting activities or clubs

13. People who provide you with services

14. The Internet

What others can you think of?

TEN WAYS TO KEEP IN TOUCH WITH YOUR NETWORK

Use the following ways to communicate with your network:

1. Letters

2. E-mail

3. Faxes

4. Phone

5. In-person meetings

6. Newsletters

7. Greeting cards

8. Photos

9. Advertising specialties

10. Breakfasts, lunches, drinks, dinners

What others can you think of?

Things to Keep In Touch About

Key events:

- New job or promotion
- Special achievement
- Birth or marriage
- Birthday or anniversary
- Graduation
- Illness
- Death

Information that might interest the people you network with:

- Articles about their work or profession
- News about them, their family, or an organization in which they may be involved

- Competitive activities
- Laws or regulations that might affect them
- Educational information
- Books or publications that may interest them
- Inquiries you receive that might be of interest to or impact someone in your network. For example, if you are a salesperson and you receive an inquiry for an item your company doesn't have but someone in your network does, recommend the inquiry to them.
- News about you, your family, or organization
- When you get a promotion
- When you achieve special recognition
- If you have created something new
- Your accomplishments
- News in general

A NETWORKING EXAMPLE

Has this ever happened to you? You are on a plane or in a hotel. You start talking to a perfect stranger. You find you have a common interest and the chemistry seems right. You exchange cards or phone numbers and wonder if you will ever hear from that person again.

When I was in China staying at the China Hotel in Guangzhou (Canton), I attended the Guangzhou Fair, trying to develop business activities. I had to give a banquet for some of the local people with whom I wanted to do business. In China, you never just have lunch—you have a banquet. Since I didn't know the custom and practice of giving a banquet, I asked to see the manager of the hotel, hoping he would guide me. The manager, a European, proved to be very helpful. He was personable, extremely knowledgeable, and accommodating. He even invited me to have a private dinner with him. We seemed to hit it off and exchanged a great deal of information. He was doing his job of cultivating a customer.

Afterward, my associate from Hong Kong and I always stayed at his hotel when we were in Guangzhou. I was still learning and appreciated his help. When we parted, we both said we would be in touch and his name went on my networking list. I knew I would be back to other fairs and that he would be sure I was treated well. He also seemed to have wide contacts. I sent him a thank you letter and put him on our newsletter list. He sent me a memorial plate of my stay at the hotel and we began a long-standing friendship. We have had dinner together with our wives. The bonus is a relationship that developed between my wife and myself and his daughter. She attended school here in New York, which gave us an opportunity to get to know her. We have become Auntie Gloria and Uncle Ed.

I have many stories of contacts made from India to Nepal, from London to Italy—contacts that have resulted in networking and that have been, personally and business-wise, richly rewarding. My experiences have proven to me that networking is an extremely strong tool that can have a major impact on your life.

12

LET'S GET DOWN TO ACTION

> *God loves to help him who strives*
> *to help himself.*
>
> —Aeschylus (525–456 B.C.)

I promised to explore with you when to take action, when to plan, and when to stop planning and begin to act. Well, here we are, at the last chapter of the book, so let's talk about the most potent tool in your arsenal—ACTION.

PLANNING TO ACT

All your dreams, planning, thinking, and talking will accomplish nothing without taking action. You will see what I mean when I tell you about a man I have mentored.

Let's call him Jim. Jim has wonderful dreams and sensible goals. He's a great researcher, analyzer, and plan developer, but something always prevents him from doing what he plans. One of his goals is to become a consultant. In fact, he does some part-time consulting while holding down a responsible executive position for a Fortune 500 company. He has his company's permission to do part-time consulting. They feel it gives him broad experience and helps him with his regular job.

When Jim retires he would like to spend his time consulting. We have talked many times about the things he should do to prepare himself to launch his full-time consulting effort. One of the things we agreed would help him toward this goal would be to have a number of articles published and, if possible, a book. To help get him started we co-authored an article. Jim has since come up with a lot of good ideas for other articles that he asked me to co-author. Although I would have liked to, it was important that he tackle them alone. For some reason, however, he never could make the leap from ideas to committing them to paper. I offered to help, once he got his thoughts down, but that also proved fruitless. He always had a good reason (I would say rationalization) for not getting down to writing. Here are some of his reasons:

- I'm too busy at work.

- I don't have the time now because I have an outside consulting assignment.

- The family is moving to a new city and there is too much preparation and too many other things to do.

- I now have to do a lot of traveling for the company.

- I started it, but family demands do not leave me time to finish it.

In my view, his reasons are excuses. There may be some psychological factors at work. Perhaps he's just too scared to commit himself to print because others may criticize him. Maybe he hasn't figured out what to say beyond the essential idea. It may also be that facing that blank sheet of paper is intimidating, or that he just can't get himself to sit down to work his ideas into form. There may be other emotional reasons that hold him back—I'm just not sure.

If Jim really lacks the time, he must somehow make the time if he really wants to build up published works. Writing an article or getting a book started requires a great deal of discipline. For me, and I know for many others, it requires setting special time aside to write. Perhaps Jim could get up an hour earlier every day to write. I recall the days when I would arrive at my office between 6:30 and 7:00 every morning. In order to write and still get to the office at my usual time, I woke up an hour earlier to get in some writing time. When I traveled, instead of reading or talking with a seat mate, I spent the time writing. I also wrote while waiting to see clients or buyers. Finding the time, even for the busiest person, is the easy part. It's getting over the emotional restraints that's so difficult.

Here is what we did to help Jim actively work on a book. First, we talked candidly about why he couldn't seem to go from idea to action. Secondly, we introduced some techniques he had not thought of to help him get his ideas organized and down on paper. He bought a small pocket tape recorder and began to talk into it every spare minute he could find. He also engaged a good editor, one who could take his ideas and notes and put them into coherent thoughts that flowed into clear sentences. What Jim needed was a "bridge" to get his thoughts down and to sort them into readable material. The tape recorder and an editor worked for him. For someone else, the bridge to action might require other aids. The point is that Jim found what helped him get over his block. The reason he found it was that he was willing to recognize that he was blocked, he discussed the problem with someone he trusted, and then utilized that assistance to help him complete what he wanted to do. Jim had to plan for what he wanted and then plan how to take action.

Here are some hints on how to plan to take action:

1. Just as you examine all aspects of your plan, examine the actions you will need to implement it.

2. Ask yourself whether you will be able to take on the actions required.

3. If you find you can't act, explore why. Make a list of the things you feel hold you back.

4. Don't hesitate to use a crutch to help you get over any impediments to action, just as Jim did.

5. Figure out how you can overcome the things that are holding you back. If you can't do it by yourself, talk with one or two people close to you. Share your concerns. Ask them what they think would help you to act.

6. Once you understand the impediments, do whatever it takes to prepare yourself to take action. It might mean help to lift psychological barriers, or it might mean partnering with someone who can do the things you can't.

ENOUGH PLANNING— IT'S TIME TO ACT

Have you ever been in this position? You hate your job. You complain to everyone how terrible your boss is and what a lousy company you work for. Yet you never do anything about it. Why do you think that is? Is change so difficult for you? Is it because of economic reasons? Do you like being in an unhappy situation? Why can't you change jobs if you're unhappy? Do you just like to complain?

Like the situation with Jim, there are usually psychological reasons why you can't act. There may also be practical reasons as well: family, earnings, not being able to move to a new location. Perhaps it's because the things you complain about are not as bad as having to make a change. You may have other reasons.

You must first analyze your situation to see if the reason is really what you think it is. Then you have to plan for change before you can take action. You can't just give up your livelihood. It feeds you and the family. First, begin to work toward replacing what you have with what will lead to what you want. In prior chapters we talked about research and planning. Taking action—getting out and doing it—is often the hardest thing to do. Years ago, when I wanted to change jobs, I couldn't get myself to take action. At the time I experienced pure fear at the possibility of not being able to find a job I would like, that it wouldn't pay enough so that we could make ends meet, or that it might not ultimately lead to my goal of going into my own business.

Here's what I did to help me make the change and overcome my fears:

- Made sure my family was behind me
- Talked with my mentors and advisors
- Planned to have enough money on reserve in case the change did not work out
- Wrote a job description of the ideal job
- Researched the work required for each new job offered
- Very carefully checked out each potential new company
- Analyzed all the research I had done once again
- Steeled myself to go through the hated process of job hunting and then do it
- Asked executives I knew to give me their opinions of my credentials and what they thought the odds were of finding what I wanted
- Prepared my résumé
- Took action

I found a new job with Lightolier, the lighting fixture company. The owners of the company were great people and treated me well. I could have had a long career with them, but the pull to be in my own business would not leave me. The experience was positive, but I knew that even working at a job I had wanted and with people I liked was not the answer for me. The job did, however, help me build my selling skills and gain the experience I needed to start our own sales agency. Ironically, years later, Lightolier became a client of our consulting company.

FIRE, READY, AIM

Opportunities that require immediate action often present themselves. You can't plan for everything or every contingency. There are times to shoot first and get ready after. Here is an example of when I had to "fire" first. At NYU I was giving the first class of a new course I had developed: "Consulting Skills and Practices." The class was supposed to role-play at selling skills. Prior to that segment we had been talking about fees. After I reviewed average fees for different types of consulting, one of the students asked what my per diem fee was. I told them what it was per day, but also that I charged fees in one of three ways: per diem, retainer, and on a project basis. I explained that often a project cost was less expensive to the client than per diem pricing because other people were assigned certain aspects of the project and the fees we billed for their services were far less than mine. I wanted them to be sure to understand that every consulting assignment was not based upon a per diem fee, that we had a team who worked on projects, and that, in fact, we advised clients to engage our services, where appropriate, on a phased project basis.

Back to the role-playing exercise: I couldn't get anyone to volunteer. Even when I called on two students, one to be the buyer and one to be the seller, they declined. Then one of them said they wanted to see how someone who could get my kind of fee was able to sell a client. They said, "You role-play for us." And so I did. One of the students, an established consultant (the class was a mix of consultants and wannabes), played the buyer. I was not prepared. I hadn't expected to be called upon in this way so I had not planned for it. Even though I had gone through real situations of selling potential clients for many years, I was concerned. I didn't know if the student playing the buyer would do all he could to put me on the spot, or worse, make it too easy. I was also concerned that the students would not get a positive experience from the exchange.

From past experience, I was prepared to react to whatever the student/buyer threw at me. But I was worried that the students would not learn as much as they would have from role-playing themselves. Happily it proved to be one of the best sessions of the course. Much to my surprise, the students learned even more than they would have from watching their fellow students role-play. I have a new class coming up soon. I plan to set up a situation where I do the role-playing and they do the commenting. I am eager to see if it can work as well when it's planned for as opposed to letting it happen spontaneously.

There are events you have been preparing for most of your life. You know more than you think you do and can act in certain situations without major preparation, providing you trust in yourself. When the situation calls for it, don't be afraid to act without planning.

SPEND YOUR TIME WISELY AND PRIORITIZE

The following story, anonymously written, has been circulating on the Internet. It makes this point: spend your time wisely and to do the "big" things first. Here is what was written:

> A while back I was reading about an expert on the subject of time management. One day this expert was speaking to a group of business students and, to drive home a point, used an illustration those students will never forget. As this man stood in front of the group of high-powered overachievers, he said, "Okay, time for a quiz." Then he pulled out a one-gallon, wide-mouthed mason jar and set it on a table in front of him. Then he produced about a dozen fist-sized rocks and carefully placed them, one at a time, into the jar.

When the jar was filled to the top and no more rocks would fit inside, he asked, "Is this jar full?" Everyone in the class said, "Yes." Then he said, "Really?" He reached under the table and pulled out a bucket of gravel. Then he dumped some gravel in and shook the jar, causing pieces of gravel to work themselves down into the spaces between the big rocks. Then he asked the group once more, "Is the jar full?" By this time the class was onto him. "Probably not," one of them answered. "Good!" he replied. He reached under the table and brought out a bucket of sand. He started dumping the sand in and it went into all the spaces left between the rocks and the gravel. Once more he asked the question, "Is this jar full?" "No!" the class shouted. Once again he said, "Good!" Then he grabbed a pitcher of water and began to pour it in until the jar was filled to the brim. Then he looked up at the class and asked, "What is the point of this illustration?"

One eager beaver raised his hand and said, "The point is, no matter how full your schedule is, if you try really hard, you can always fit some more things into it!"

"No," the speaker replied, "that's not the point. The truth this illustration teaches us is: If you don't put the big rocks in first, you'll never get them in at all."

What are the big rocks in your life? A project that you want to accomplish? Time with your loved ones? Your faith, your education, your finances? A cause? Teaching or mentoring others? Remember to put these big rocks in first or you'll never get them in at all. So, tonight or in the morning when you are reflecting on this short story, ask yourself this question: What are the big rocks in my life or business? Then, put those in your jar first.

Note: This was sent to me by Ron Leder, Cooper Leder Marketing, Inc., 3000 Marcus Avenue, Lake Success, NY 11042; http://www.clmweb.com).

You have to know which are your big rocks, the ones that go in first in your jar of life. You can figure it out if you plan, or you may know it intuitively. It might be that the first big rock in your life is family. Whatever affects the family's well-being should get loaded in first. The second rock to load in could be things that affect your work or profession. Life, however, is full of much more than just family and work. So then comes the gravel of life, then the sand, and then the water. The point is this: know which is which and then prioritize so you can act on the most important things first.

HOW MUCH DO YOU WANT TO EARN?

One of the first questions I ask a client or an individual I'm trying to help is what they expect to earn in five, ten, and twenty years from now. Often they have never thought about it. Yet all your current plans will impact what you want to earn in the future. You must plan how to achieve these earnings or they will remain mere dreams. Most important, put the plan into action. Only then will you have the best possible chance of achieving the earnings you want. Here are some questions to ask yourself in order to analyze whether or not you're on the right track:

- Do you indeed know what you want to earn in five, ten, and twenty years from now? That much? Really? Well, that sounds doable. So, how will you achieve it?

- Are you only dreaming of what you would like to earn or do you have a plan?

- Is your plan in writing?

- Are you constantly acting on your plan?

- What action do you have to take today?

- What action should you take tomorrow?

- What actions are needed in the future?

- Have you set a budget for applying your resources to your action?

BUDGETING

Years ago, a friend and business associate of mine and I took a business trip around the world together. We had planned the trip carefully, budgeted the dollars we would spend, even how we would spend our time in each of the countries we were visiting. Appointments were set up in advance and reconfirmed. We also planned recreation time. Most important, we knew exactly what our goals were for the trip. I also had to work the cost of the trip into our business budget for the year. We had to figure out the value of spending the money on the trip or spending it on something else. What would we gain? What could we lose? Consideration had to be given to the time and possible money loss by not being available to contact customers and clients while we were away. I was not only budgeting our dollars for the trip, but also my time and energy.

THREE WAYS TO SET YOUR BUDGET FOR LIVING

Thought must be given to budgeting your money, just as *consideration* must be given to budgeting your time and energy. Consider the following:

MONEY

- How much money will be required to accomplish the project, event, or plan?

- How much money is actually available?

- Are you sure that you are allotting the correct amount of money to do the job?

- Why are you investing your money in this?

- Over what period of time have you budgeted for?

- Would dollars be more productively spent on something else?

- How will you monitor your budget to make sure you don't under or overspend?

TIME

- How much time will be needed for this event, project, or plan?

- Are you sure that you are allotting the right amount of time to do the job?

- How much time do you actually have available?

- Why are you investing your time in this event, project, or plan?

- What do you hope to gain?

- Over what period of time have you budgeted for?

- Would your time be more productively spent on something else?

- How will you monitor your time budget to make sure you don't under- or over-allot your time?

ENERGY

- How much energy will be required for this event, project, or plan?

- Are you sure about the amount of energy needed to do the job?

- How much energy do you actually think you have to invest?

- Why are you investing your energy in this?

- What return do you expect for the energy expended?

- Over what period of time will you need to expend this energy?

- Would your energy be more productively spent on something else?

- How will you monitor your budget to make sure you don't under- or over-allot your energy?

It is obvious that the questions for these three investments are virtually the same. But they are questions you need to answer before you swing into action. Far too often we undertake projects because they sound good, only to find that they drain us of money, time, or energy. Be aware and invest wisely.

LIVE BY YOUR BUDGET

It takes discipline and planning to live by the budgets we set. I admit that I have not always established budgets for some personal plans. Sometimes it isn't necessary. But most of the time it's desirable to know what to plan in terms of dollars, time, and energy. The plans you devise and the actions you take to implement your plan become more realistic when you have calculated and thought about these factors. The Goal Planning form in Chapter 6 did not include these factors. The form on the next page does.

COMPETITION, COMPETITION, EVERYWHERE YOU TURN

> *Thou shalt not covet, but tradition*
> *Approves all forms of competition.*

—Arthur Hugh Clough (1819–1861)
The Latest Decalogue (1862) l.19

When you were a teenager, do you recall how much time you spent thinking about how to win the object of your affection? When I was in high school another fellow and I competed for the affections of a classmate. He and I were friends and in the same fraternity. Nevertheless, when it came to the young woman, the competition was keen. If there was a fraternity dance, we would each try to get to the phone before the other in order to be the one to get a date. I think my proudest day in high school was when she accepted my fraternity pin and became my steady girlfriend.

Form for Developing Goals and Strategies plus Dollars, Time, and Energy

GOAL _____

RANK _____

COMPLETION DATE _____

Strategy	Person(s) Responsi- ble	Date to be Accom- plished	What Will It Cost?	Time Spent	Energy Spent	Return	How to Measure	Rank

Well, starting from those teenage days of ours to today, we have always had to fight for what we want. Sometimes we do it by planning, other times by taking quick action. There are times when it requires a combination of both planning and quick action. The point is: in our society, even if you are a person who would rather live cooperatively and not combatively, you will be forced to compete and fight for what you want. It's just a matter of degree as to how competitive you will have to be to successfully meet your goals.

Because there is competition everywhere you turn, you have to take it into account when you plan. Also, you may often have to act very quickly when faced with competition. Competition may come from two or more sources. They want what you want; they compete with you for it. It's a rivalry. It may be someone competing for the same job, for someone of the opposite sex, a place at a university, in business, in the same profession, or for anything you want that others want, too. Therefore, be continually aware of who your competition is and what their strengths and weaknesses are. In business or in the professions, you need an ongoing method for monitoring what your competition are doing. Be alert to competitive activity and have the means to track it. Some competition can be tracked by monitoring:

- your network
- rumors

- publications
- financial information
- community activities
- want ads
- friends
- acquaintances
- Internet
- colleagues
- anything else that will help give you a full picture of your competition

Does it matter that you have competition? In most situations, it does. In others, it doesn't. I have always contended that, in our consulting practice, we have no competition. No matter that there may be hundreds of companies that offer the same or similar services as we do, no one can implement those services as we do. On the other hand, we can't implement the same services in the same way that others do. Since we often go after the same client, you would have to say that we have competition. Just as there may be no one who can do things quite the way you do, there is still competition with those who claim to produce the same or better results or who have a better way of doing whatever you offer.

Each and every one of us has a special quality that allows us to do things differently. Yet we compete with the product we have to offer—ourselves.

Years from Now?

I expect that most of the readers of this book will be people much younger than I am and I imagine there will also be a few readers of my generation who seek to change their lives and will, therefore, also find this book of value. Whether you are the younger reader or are my contemporary, we all think about the years ahead and about what to do with the rest of our lives. My prayer is that you will be granted years of health so that you can work your plan, achieve your goals, and find joy and happiness in the life you choose for yourself.

Keep well, be happy, and prosper.

INDEX

A

ABCs of life, 211–18
accountants, 128–29
action
    budgeting money, time, and energy, 270–73, 274
    overcoming obstacles to, 257–60, 262–64
    planning for, 261
    putting first things first, 266–68
    reacting to the unexpected, 264–66
    responding to competition, 273, 275–76
    See also planning
Adams, Henry Brooks, 179
adversity, overcoming, 27
advertising agencies, 129
advisors
    importance of using, 128–29
    proper role of, 205–8
Aeschylus, 257
American Cancer Society, 165
anger, 81–82
Apple Computer, 196–97
Aristotle, 213, 231
Arthritis Foundation, 115, 164–65
At Home in The Universe: The Search for the Laws of Self-Organization and Complexity, 75, 180
attorneys, 129

B

C

P

paradigms
   breaking, 186, 189–92
   definition of, 185
   examples of changing, 192–96
   impact on our perceptions, 186–89
   See also problem-solving
Paradigms: The Business of Discovering the Future, 192–94
peace, achieving inner. *See* balance, achieving personal
Peale, Norman Vincent, 211
persistence, 212, 214, 216–17, 218
personal balance. *See* balance, achieving personal
personal mission statements. *See* mission statements, personal
personal responsibility. *See* responsibility, personal
Peters, Tom, 180
physiological needs, 33–36
planning
   analyzing strengths, weaknesses, opportunities, and threats, 146–48
   assembling the final document, 155–59
   computer software for, 151
   content *vs.* process, 92–93
   contingency planning, 139–41
   deciding where you want to be, 96–97
   defining success, 101–2
   determining costs, 100
   developing strategies, 97–98
   facing reality, 135–39
   for future earnings, 269
   getting help from others, 98–100
   importance of, 12–13, 50, 89–90, 91–92, 159–60
   importance of research, 144–46
   keeping plans succinct, 110–11
   knowing your starting point, 95–96
   LifePlan system, 89–92
   making assumptions, 141–42
   monitoring progress, 130–32
   networking, 98–100
   Never Ending Planning Cycle, 93–94
   questions to ask, 95–102
   reality check questions, 138–39